CHAM

ADULT LEARNERS' WRITING GUIDE

by

Ruth Thornton

CHAMBERS

CHAMBERS

An imprint of Chambers Harrap Publishers Ltd
7 Hopetoun Crescent
Edinburgh, EH7 4AY

First published by Chambers Harrap Publishers Ltd 2006

A CIP catalogue record for this book is available from the British Library.

ISBN-13: 978 0550 10187 7
ISBN-10: 0550 10187 X

Editor: Ian Brookes
Editorial Consultant: Martin Cutts
Publishing Manager: Patrick White
Prepress: David Reid

Designed and typeset by Chambers Harrap Publishers Ltd, Edinburgh
Printed in Italy by Legoprint

Contents

Acknowledgements

I'd like to thank all the people who have helped me with this book. Some listened, some read, some made comments and suggestions, some encouraged and some cajoled. A big thank you to them all. Here are some of their names:

Chris, Alex and Nick; Suzanne Bardgett; Chris Defty; Sally Easton; Lynne Franks; Jane Griffith; Kate Hardy; Cathy Macadam; Caroline Molyneux; Rupert Pitt; William Thornton; Carol Wilson.

I would particularly like to thank Martin Cutts, research director of the Plain Language Commission, who devised the PROCESS method. Details of the method are set out in the book with his permission.

This book is dedicated to Joan and Jim Taylor and Marjorie Bye in thanks for their years of support and encouragement.

Introduction

ABOUT THIS BOOK

Chambers Adult Learners' Writing Guide has been developed in response to demand from teachers of adult literacy for a book which addresses the needs of adult learners.

Many adults lack confidence about expressing themselves in writing, and many are taking steps to acquire the skills that will help them write more effectively. This book has been designed with such people in mind. It aims to help adult learners approach practical writing tasks with more confidence – whether these tasks involve composing an e-mail, filling out a form or writing a job application – so that they can communicate effectively and without barriers when they need to write to their friends, their children's teachers, their employers or other people in authority.

The appearance of the book has been designed with this aim in mind. The book has an open and attractive layout with colour used to highlight special information. The typeface used has the approval of the British Dyslexia Association.

The contents of the book have also been carefully designed to help the adult learner: vocabulary is kept simple, but is relevant to the needs of adult life; the book does not attempt to explain language in all its complexity but focuses on the key ideas that learners really need to understand; and whenever a new idea is explained, the explanation is followed by plenty of exercises so that learners can test themselves repeatedly until they are confident that they understand the idea correctly.

These features make this book suitable to be used either as a self-study tool or in combination with adult education programmes.

HOW TO USE THIS BOOK

If you think this book looks too big for you to read it all at once, I have some good news for you. You don't have to.

The really important part of this book – the part that helps you prepare for the essential writing tasks of adult life – is to be found in parts D and E on pages 119 to 196. These sections form the heart of this book and will give you a practical approach that you can follow whatever you are writing. Everyone who uses this book should read these parts of it.

However, the book also addresses some essential points about the English language that you will need to understand if you are to write clearly and effectively. These points are covered in parts A, B and C on pages 9 to 118. Most readers will find some useful information in these parts of the book, but you may well already understand some of the basic ideas that are explained there. So to help you work out which parts of the book will be helpful to you, you should try to complete the Language Quiz on pages 1 to 8. The Language Quiz has been specially designed to pinpoint which aspects of English you already understand and which ones you are not sure about. If you have trouble with any of the sections of the Language Quiz, you can go to the part of the book that explains more about the idea covered by that section of the quiz.

The explanations that you will find in parts A, B and C include plenty of exercises that you can do to see if you have understood the idea correctly. 'Quick Check' exercises have the answers printed underneath the questions. You should get into the habit of masking the answers – you can use your hand, a ruler or a piece of paper – until you have done the question, and then unmasking the answer to see if you were correct. After you have done the 'Quick Check' exercises, you can really test yourself by having a go at some further questions which don't have the answers printed underneath. But you can still check how you well did on these additional exercises by checking the answers on pages 197 to 244 at the back of the book.

By practising until you are confident that you understand, you will improve your language skills and build up a picture of how sentences work. You will find that you will use these skills every time that you write.

After you have finished working through this book, keep it around so that you can refer to it whenever you have to write something. Parts A, B and C will refresh your memory about key points of grammar and punctuation and about words that are easily confused, while part E gives you handy advice for many of the specific types of writing that you may have to do.

I hope that after using this book you will be able to approach the task of writing with real confidence.

Language Quiz

This quiz contains 90 questions to test your understanding of the important points about the English language that are explained in the first part of this book.

The purpose of the quiz is to help you recognize which bits of the book will be most useful to you. Each group of questions routes you to a part of the book that can give you explanations, examples and some exercises. If you can do a part of the quiz easily, there's no need to study the explanations and do the exercises. But if you're not sure about any of the key ideas involved, then you'll know where to go to find out more.

You may like to do the quiz in sections or all at once. As you go through the quiz, tick the numbers of those pages you think you will need to read through later.

You can check your answers to the quiz on pages 199–201.

PART A THE BASICS OF GRAMMAR

Do you know what to call it?
Do you know what the key words to describe language are? You need to know them to be able to explain why what you've written is right.

Q.1–5: Which word in each sentence is a verb?

1 He ran down the road as fast as possible.
a. road **b. possible** **c. ran**

2 They decided on a new method.
a. decided **b. method** **c. new**

3 She loves skipping along the sandy beach.
a. skipping **b. she** **c. loves**

4 The new management team opted for flexible working hours for all.
a. opted **b. team** **c. working**

5 The rescue team arrived on the scene just in time.
a. time **b. rescue** **c. arrived**

➤ *Not sure about verbs? Check pages 12–21.*

Q.6–10: Which word in each sentence is a noun?

6 He ran down the road as fast as possible.
a. road **b. possible** **c. ran**

7 They sat and read in the garden happily.
a. read **b. happily** **c. garden**

8 The light shone brightly.
a. shone **b. light** **c. brightly**

9 Please tell him I need some help.
a. help **b. need** **c. tell**

10 Do you have a spare pen I could borrow, please?
a. pen **b. spare** **c. borrow**

➤ *Not sure about nouns? Check pages 22–7.*

Q.11–15: *Which word in each sentence is an adjective?*

11 Please could you show me the way to the green room?
a. please **b. way** **c. green**

12 Where have all the new chairs been put?
a. chair **b. where** **c. new**

13 Their holiday in Spain was expensive.
a. their **b. holiday** **c. expensive**

14 The teacher has asked him to move the heavy books.
a. teacher **b. heavy** **c. move**

15 Their friends arrived for the weekend at the remote cottage.
a. remote **b. weekend** **c. arrived**

➤ *Not sure about adjectives? Check pages 28–30.*

Q.16–20: *Which word in each sentence is an adverb?*

16 He walked enthusiastically into school on the first day.
a. school **b. walked** **c. enthusiastically**

17 Sitting in the shady park they ate their picnic slowly.
a. slowly **b. picnic** **c. shady**

18 He worked on the project methodically.
a. project **b. worked** **c. methodically**

19 Chris willingly offered his help putting up the tent.
a. offered **b. willingly** **c. putting up**

20 At Live8 people gave generously.
a. people **b. generously** **c. gave**

➤ *Not sure about adverbs? Check pages 31–5.*

Q.21–25: Which word in each sentence is the (grammatical) subject?

21 Alex took a tremendous catch in the match.
a. Alex **b. match** **c. tremendous**

22 The managers agreed a new working policy.
a. policy **b. managers** **c. agreed**

23 The school invited parents to an open evening.
a. parents **b. school** **c. evening**

24 He picked up the radio and took it into the kitchen.
a. radio **b. he** **c. picked**

25 The cats ran into the house for their tea.
a. ran **b. tea** **c. cats**

➤ *Not sure about subjects? Check page 36.*

Q.26–30: Which word in each sentence is the (grammatical) object?

26 We picked up a hitchhiker on the way to the coast.
a. coast **b. we** **c. hitchhiker**

27 When we were children we ate an apple every day.
a. apple **b. day** **c. ate**

28 They bought an inflatable boat at the seaside.
a. boat **b. bought** **c. seaside**

29 The managers announced their new policy on lateness.
a. policy **b. lateness** **c. managers**

30 He ate his sandwich in silence.
a. sandwich **b. ate** **c. silence**

➤ *Not sure about objects? Check pages 37–8.*

Q.31–35: In each sentence underline the pronoun.

31 She wanted to invite her friends to the house.

32 The teacher asked me to pass the book to my friend.

33 Where did you get such thick paper?

34 They asked the group to meet at the pub.

35 Take these extra tickets for them.

➤ *Not sure about pronouns? Check pages 51–5.*

Do you know how words work correctly together?

You've now looked at the labels for things in grammar – but do you know how words fit together according to the rules? As you work through, keep in mind whether you're guessing or whether you really know. Knowing if it's right or wrong is one thing – knowing why is another!

Q.36–44: Verbs – are these sentences grammatically correct?

36 She don't eat chocolate at all.

37 The players agree with the pay cuts.

38 Don't Philip want to join in?

39 They said they was happy to leave early.

40 She come to visit us two weeks ago.

41 They have wrote to me every day since they left.

42 He's ate all his supper.

43 She's ran round the track twice.

44 Have they swam in the sea yet this year?

➤ *Not sure about how verbs work? Check pages 40–50.*

Q.45–49: Adverbs and adjectives – are these sentences grammatically correct?

45 What a match! The team played brilliant!

46 That is a superb painting.

47 He reads rather slow.

48 They can run fast.

49 You dance nice.

➤ *Not sure about how adverbs and adjectives work? Check pages 34–5.*

Q.50–54: Pronouns – are these sentences grammatically correct?

50 The school has changed the timetable. They want the day to start later.

51 The Government have increased spending on education. They recognize how important it is to the electorate.

52 The cats ran down the path. It looked very contented.

53 My friend and me went on holiday together last year.

54 The boss asked Julia and I to take the minutes at the meeting.

➤ *Not sure about how pronouns work? Check pages 51–60.*

Q.55–59: Are these complete sentences?

55 He doesn't enjoy driving.

56 The final recommendations from the report.

57 He going on holiday at the end of the month.

58 Hurriedly finished eating and left the room.

59 They need help with this.

➤ *Not sure what makes a complete sentence? Check pages 61–4.*

PART B GOOD PUNCTUATION

Q.60: Where do the full stops go in this paragraph?

60 Alex and Nick wandered home from the park they had had a great afternoon playing with their friends they intended to have a quick supper and finish their homework unfortunately when they got home around 6pm supper wasn't ready.

➤ *Not sure about full stops? Check pages 68–71.*

Q.61–62: Where do the question marks go?

61 Where did you spend the last week in January.

62 He asked me how much I wanted to spend on the MP3 player.

➤ *Not sure about question marks? Check pages 72–3.*

Q.63: Where do the exclamation marks go?

63 That's an absolutely amazing dog. I've never seen one so huge.

➤ *Not sure about exclamation marks? Check page 74.*

Q.64–66: Where do the commas go?

64 He bought butter margarine sugar salt and flour.

65 Liz my best friend from school keeps in touch regularly.

66 If you want to help the students learn the subject yourself first.

➤ *Not sure about commas? Check pages 75–81.*

Q.67–68: Where do the colons (and commas) go?

67 He told us what we'd learn how to drill the right size holes in a wall how to use Rawlplugs and how to put up a shelf.

68 Bring everything you'll need for a week in freezing conditions warm underwear thick sweaters and trousers decent walking boots and a thick waterproof coat with a hood.

➤ *Not sure about colons? Check pages 82–3.*

Q.69–74: Where do the apostrophes go?

69 Im not sure if hes coming to the meal this evening or even if youre coming.

70 The teachers reports were stacked high in the classrooms.

71 The managers decision has made everyone unhappy.

72 The dogs dinners in its bowl.

73 Its never too late to change.

74 That tables got to go – its almost falling apart its so unsafe.

➤ *Not sure about apostrophes? Check pages 84–9.*

PART C EASILY CONFUSED WORDS

Q.75–90: What is the right word to use?

75 Do you ______ who you are?
a. now **b.** know **c.** no

76 It can't ______ been him.
a. off **b.** of **c.** have

77 It's ______ nice here.
a. quite **b.** quiet

78 ______ books are definitely the best.
a. they're **b.** there **c.** their

79 What's she going to ______ tonight?
a. where **b.** wear **c.** we're **d.** were

80 ______ bag is this?
a. whose **b.** who's

81 Have you ______ your kids?
a. bought **b.** brought

82 You need to ______ cracking eggs.
a. practice **b.** practise

83 The council refused to grant him a ______.
a. licence **b.** license

84 Why can't you ______ their offer of help?
a. except **b.** accept **c.** expect

85 He has no ______ but to find a new job.
a. alternate **b.** alternative

86 Please ______ me your sweater.
a. borrow **b.** lend

87 The Holocaust Exhibition had a deep ______ on him.
a. effect **b.** affect

88 She has ______ on the sofa all day.
a. laid **b.** lain **c.** lied

89 The doctor told him to ______ deeply.
a. breadth **b.** breath **c.** breathe

90 The car was ______ when she rode into it.
a. stationery **b.** stationary

➤ *Not sure about some of these? Check pages 93–118.*

PART A
THE BASICS OF GRAMMAR

Why do I need to know about grammar?

Writing is more difficult than talking. When we talk to people, they can tell us if they don't understand clearly and give us a chance to explain what we mean. But when we write, we probably won't be there to explain if the reader doesn't understand. So it's important that we make ourselves clear.

Luckily, there is a set of rules about language that we and our readers can both follow. If we do this, we can get our message across without it being misunderstood.

We often use the word 'grammar' to talk about these rules. The good news is that we're not aiming to cover the whole of English grammar here – just enough to help you understand what you are trying to do when you write.

What do I need to know about grammar?

What we will do is look at a few key points that we need to understand before we can explain why something is right or wrong. These will help us see how English is meant to work and check whether our writing follows the rules.

These key ideas are:

- verbs
- nouns
- adjectives
- adverbs
- subjects and objects
- using the right form of the verb
- pronouns
- complete sentences

Once we understand these ideas and we understand how sentences work and how they fit together, we can avoid some of the most basic errors in our writing.

Key idea 1: Verbs

At school I was taught 'a verb is a doing word'. I could – and frequently did – recite that phrase, usually in a dull chant with the thirty other kids in my class in primary school. And I've met thousands of other people who were taught exactly the same description of a verb.

But although I could recite the phrase, if you had shown me some writing and asked me to point out the verbs I would not have been able to do it.

So what *is* a verb?

Another way to think about verbs is to say they are **time–action words**. They tell us about an *action* and they usually give us an idea of *when the action happens* – in the past, in the present or in the future.

Let's look at a sentence:

They ran down the hill.

Here the word *ran* is the verb, the time–action word. *Ran* tells us two things:

- **the action** – something to do with running
- **the time** it happened – the past

Let's look at another sentence:

I see you.

Here the word *see* is the verb, the time–action word. *See* tells us two things:

- **the action** – something to do with seeing
- **the time** it is happening – now

Quick check

Mask the answers with your hand or a piece of paper and underline the verb in each sentence below. Remember that you're looking for the word that tells about an action and when it happens. Unmask the text and check your answers.

1 John ate all the sandwiches.

ate

2 I ran home.

ran

3 The children played tennis.

played

4 Chris weeded the garden.

weeded

5 Nick drinks hot chocolate in the morning.

drinks

6 The keeper caught the ball.

caught

7 The sun rises at 6am.

rises

8 Buds appear on almond trees in February.

appear

9 The kingfishers flew along the river.

flew

10 Many trees lose their leaves in autumn.

lose

Some verbs are made up of more than one word

In the sentences we have looked at so far, the verb has been a single word:

He *eats* at 7pm.

But in some sentences, the idea of time and action involves extra words. These may help to describe when the action takes place or how sure we are about the action.

He *is eating* some cheese.
He *might eat* fish.
He *had eaten* before our arrival.

In the first sentence, *is eating* is the verb and tells us what he's doing now. In the second sentence, *might eat* is the verb and shows us we're not sure whether he eats fish. In the third sentence, *had eaten* is the verb and shows us he ate before our arrival.

Let's look at another sentence. Can you spot the verb?

It will rain tomorrow.

Here the two words *will rain* make up the verb. The words *will rain* tell us:

- **the action** – something to do with raining
- **the time** it will happen – the future

Let's look at one more:

It might have rained yesterday.

Here three words make up the verb. The words *might have rained* tell us:

- **the action** – something to do with raining
- **the time** this might have happened – here in the past
- that we're not sure if it rained or not (indicated by the word *might*)

Quick check

Mask the answers. Take a look at these sentences and underline the verb. Remember that a verb can be made up of more than one word. Unmask the text and check your answers.

1 They finished the book.

finished

2 Lisa will play the saxophone after school tomorrow.

will play

3 He might have eaten all the doughnuts.

might have eaten

4 The film is starting now.

is starting

5 The complaint was made at 10pm.

was made

6 Bart was reading a new comic.

was reading

7 The sun never sets in summer in the Arctic Circle.

sets

8 The photos were published without permission.

were published

We need extra words to make questions and negatives

We often need extra words to go with the verb when we are asking questions or making negative statements (saying something is not the case).

The words *does* and *do* help us make questions about now, the present time.

Does he like doughnuts?
Do you like doughnuts?
Do I like doughnuts?

We use the word *did* when we ask questions about the past time.

Did he work in that office?
Did they give him the job?

We use *does not* and *do not* to make a negative when we are talking about the present.

He *does not* go to school yet.
They *do not* want any flowers in their garden.

We use *did not* to make a negative when talking about the past.

They *did not* arrive until 8pm.

Quick check

Mask the answers and underline the verbs in each sentence. Unmask the text and check your answers.

1 He didn't see his friend at the bus stop.

didn't + see

2 Where does he live?

does + live

3 Do you eat tomatoes?

do + eat

4 He does not do his work well.

does + not + do

5 They didn't buy any furniture.

didn't + buy

Now really test yourself

Underline the verbs – the time–action words – in these sentences. You can check your answers on page 202.

1 John ordered two beers and a glass of red wine.

2 The kids ran down the hill at top speed.

3 Alex was running into school when the bell rang.

4 Peter said he had put the shopping in the fridge.

5 The meal should have been ready hours ago.

6 The tickets were sold as soon as they appeared.

7 He didn't watch the TV programme.

8 They have finished the book already.

9 They were helping their friends.

10 When are they leaving?

11 He might have gone to the coast.

12 You must finish the curtains by lunchtime.

13 Ros has just phoned me about her daughter's exam results.

14 The windows were cleaned last Thursday.

15 The director couldn't understand the problem.

16 He applied for the job and got it.

Some verbs don't look like action words

If you got all of those right, you have understood the main idea of verbs. But before we leave the subject of verbs, we'll look at a couple of finer points about them. For example, which word would you underline as the verb in this sentence?

Bart is happy.

If you've underlined *is*, you're right. But *is* doesn't seem much like a 'doing word' or a 'time–action word'.

It is a verb, though – it describes how something or someone is, rather than what he or she does. *Is* is not the only verb that doesn't look like an action word. Look for the verbs in following sentences:

He feels sick.
They don't know the alphabet yet.
The table looks new.

Did you spot that *feels*, *know* and *looks* were verbs?

These verbs are like *is* – they describe how someone is rather than what they are doing.

Quick check

Mask the answers and underline the verbs in each sentence. Unmask the text and check your answers.

1 He seemed happy.

seemed

2 Alex understands about electricity.

understands

3 Anne appeared quite happy.

appeared

4 They considered him the best person for the job.

considered

5 The salad looks delicious.

looks

Some sentences have more than one verb

There does not have to be just one verb in a sentence. Sometimes more than one action is being described, and so there will be more than one verb.

For example, one thing may be happening after another.

Marco *ran* home and *put* the kettle on.
They *went* into the mountains and *camped* for a month.

In the first sentence, *ran* and *put* are both verbs and tell us the two different things Marco did. In the second sentence, *went* and *camped* are both verbs.

Another reason for having more than one verb is that one thing may happen because of, instead of, or in spite of another thing.

Marco *ran* home because he *had forgotten* his keys.
They *walked* into the town even though it *was raining*.

In the first sentence, *ran* and *had forgotten* are both verbs. In the second sentence, *walked* and *was raining* are both verbs.

Sometimes, there is a main verb that is immediately followed by a second verb. Let's look at an example:

They *decided to cancel* the order.

The main action taking place is described by the word *decided*. But there is a second action – *to cancel* – that depends on *decided*. *To cancel* is called an 'infinitive'. You can recognize an infinitive because it has the word *to* in front of it.

It is quite common in English for a verb to be followed by a second verb in the infinitive.

They *wanted to go* home.
He *asked to start* early.

Quick check

Mask the answers and underline the verbs in each sentence. Unmask the text and check your answers.

1 Some passengers feel nervous whenever they fly.
feel, fly

2 He dug the garden over, raked it and then planted the seeds.
dug, raked, planted

3 Have you tried to read that book?
tried, to read

4 The children went to the park, played tennis and cycled home.
went, played, cycled

5 They wanted to meet me at the station.
wanted, to meet

6 The manager told them he had chosen the team for the match.
told, had chosen

7 The lads practised hard and ended the evening with a run round the track.
practised, ended

8 Alex took the train to Marseille and went by boat from there to Corsica.
took, went

9 He decided to look for their dog.
decided, to look for

10 He said he wanted to leave the course, but his tutor persuaded him to stay.
said, wanted, to leave, persuaded, to stay

Now really test yourself

Underline all the verbs in the following sentences. Check your answers on pages 202–3.

1 The dog chased the cats.

2 The sausages are being cooked.

3 Mira and her friend will arrive before 8pm.

4 John must announce the team soon.

5 We'll meet up next week.

6 They wanted to celebrate the occasion.

7 Eat plenty of fresh fruit.

8 Cut down on the doughnuts!

9 Any decision should be checked carefully.

10 They need to learn their lines by Saturday.

11 She couldn't have predicted their reaction.

12 He seemed genuinely surprised about the robbery.

13 She felt sorry for him.

14 They must have taken their parents' car.

Checklist

- You can think of a verb as a time–action word. It tells us about an action and when it happened: *ran; is running; finished; decides; will run*.
- Some verbs describe a state rather than an action: *she'll* ***be*** *here soon; he* ***is*** *exhausted; he* ***looks*** *tired; why* ***isn't*** *she happy?*
- The words *does*, *do* and *did* can help us make questions.
- *Does not*, *do not* and *did not* help us make negative statements.
- Some sentences have more than one verb: *they* ***wanted*** *to* ***resign***; *we* ***decided*** *to* ***meet*** *at 6pm; Felix* ***wondered*** *who his friends* ***were***; *they* ***ate***, ***drank*** *and* ***danced*** *all night*.

Key idea 2: Nouns

At school I learned that a noun was 'a person, place or thing'. This is a useful basic definition, and it helps me spot the nouns in the following sentence:

Jane found her ring in Paris.

In this sentence *Jane*, *ring* and *Paris* are nouns. *Jane* is a person, *ring* is a thing and *Paris* is a place.

(Notice that when a noun is the name of a particular person, place or thing, it is spelt with a capital letter, as in *Jane* and *Paris*, but when it is the name of a general kind of thing it does not have a capital letter, as in *ring*.)

Another way to think about nouns is to say they are labels for things – or places or people. Wherever you are reading this book there will be many nouns around you. What things can you see? The nouns *table*, *book*, *knee*, *window*, *passengers*, *raincoats* and *sky* could be the labels for some of those things you can see.

Quick check

Mask the answers and underline the nouns – people, places and things – in each sentence. Unmask the text and check your answers.

1 John saw the book on the shelf.

John, book, shelf

2 Alex rode his bicycle down the street

Alex, bicycle, street

3 The managers approved the pay-rise.

managers, pay-rise

4 Peter got the job.

Peter, job

5 Cathy and Suzanne prepared a delicious dinner.

Cathy, Suzanne, dinner

6 Usha invited her friends to lunch.

Usha, friends, lunch

Another way of identifying nouns

We have seen that the words for things we can see are nouns. However, the names of things we can't see or touch are also nouns. For example, *idea*, *pain* and *decision* are all nouns, even though we can't see an idea or a decision.

So the definition of 'a person, place or thing' is not quite as helpful as it might be. Another test for identifying nouns is that you can often put the words *the*, *an* and *a* in front of nouns.

A *car* has been stolen.
Where's the *boy* gone?

We can also use the words *the*, *an* and *a* in front of things we can't see that are nouns.

He had a *pain* in his leg.
They were unable to make the *decision*.

But if we put the words *the*, *an* and *a* in front of a verb, it doesn't make sense.

A has been stolen.
Where's the gone?

We know something's missing and that something is the noun – the person, place or thing – we're talking about.

Quick check

Mask the answers and underline any nouns you find in these sentences. Remember nouns are labels for people, places and things (and you may not be able to see or touch the things). Unmask the text and check your answers.

1 They reached an agreement about the house.

agreement, house

2 Their determination led to the success of the project.

determination, success, project

3 His mood improved when the sun came out.

mood, sun

4 She wanted to be left in peace.

peace

Now really test yourself

Underline all the nouns in the following sentences. Check your answers on pages 203–4.

1 Lisa wanted to start school early.

2 The oranges were in the bowl.

3 The holidays were over far too quickly.

4 The manager arranged the meeting for 9 June.

5 They finished the job in the time agreed.

6 The marathon raised thousands of pounds for charity.

7 His confidence was shaken by the appraisal.

8 The development of the residential area has created problems for the town.

9 Philip treated his employees to a meal every January.

10 The Eden Project makes a memorable day out.

11 He hoped he'd win the race.

12 The teachers were sure she would pass her exams.

13 Why hasn't he finished his project yet?

14 After the nightmare she didn't want to go out.

15 Harriet wanted to go to university.

Checklist

- You can think of a noun as a label for a person, place or thing: *man, park, chair, bill*.
- When a noun is the name of a particular person, place or thing, it starts with a capital letter: *Shakespeare, London, Rio Grande*.
- The words *the, a* and *an* often come before nouns.
- Some things we can't see or touch are also nouns: *an idea, the discussion, happiness*.

Quick check

Mask the right-hand column and decide which words in this list are nouns and which are verbs. Unmask the right-hand column and check your answer.

car	noun
fruit	noun
eat	verb
electricity	noun
banana	noun
write	verb
sit	verb
tree	noun
bird	noun
sew	verb

Mask the answers and pick out the nouns and the verbs in each sentence. Unmask the text and check your answers.

1 The decision was rejected by the new manager.
nouns: decision, manager; verb: was rejected

2 A child was running across the park.
nouns: child, park; verb: was running

3 My team won the cup!
nouns: team, cup; verb: won

4 He read the book rapidly and enjoyed it.
noun: book; verbs: read, enjoyed

5 Our garden is full of weeds.
nouns: garden, weeds; verb: is

6 The dog's teeth were sharp.
nouns: dog, teeth; verb: were

7 John dreamed he had got the job.
nouns: John, job; verbs: dreamed, had got

8 Sarah has stripped the wallpaper off the bathroom with a steamer.
nouns: Sarah, wallpaper, bathroom, steamer; verb: has stripped

More on nouns and verbs

The same word can sometimes be a noun **and** a verb. Look at the word *help*:

They *help* me every week.
Thank you for your *help*.

In the first sentence the word *help* is a verb. In the second sentence it is a noun.

Now think about this question: is the word *elbow* a noun or a verb?

If you said that it's a noun, you're correct, because an *elbow* can be a thing.

When I fell I grazed my *elbow*.

But if you said verb, you're correct too. *Elbow* is a time–action word in this sentence:

Some people always *elbow* their way to the front of the queue.

So if you said both noun and verb, you get top marks!

It is not enough to see each word in isolation and decide whether it's a noun or a verb. You should always look at what the word is doing in the sentence. Some words – as we've just seen with *elbow* and *help* – can be both noun and verb.

Quick check

Mask the answers and decide if the word *head* is a noun or a verb in each sentence. Unmask the text and check your answers.

1 His head is too big.

noun

2 He headed the ball into the back of the net.

verb

3 They head off to the library at 8 o'clock every morning.

verb

4 Phil has been chosen to head up the new department.

verb

5 Phil has been chosen as the new head of department.

noun

Now really test yourself

Which words are nouns and which are verbs in the following sentences? Check your answers on page 204.

1. The rescue took five hours.
2. The fireman rescued the cat in under ten minutes.
3. The saw had been tested and was extremely sharp.
4. Lisa saw all the doughnuts disappear.
5. The PIN number was on a slip of paper.
6. Don't slip on that patch of ice over there.
7. I patched up those old trousers.
8. My fingers are too long for these gloves.
9. She fingered the material.
10. The drink was made of brandy, crème de cacao and cream.
11. What would you like to drink?
12. It took him seven hours to swim the channel.
13. The report announced James should channel his energies into his art.
14. The damage will cost £500 to repair.
15. Who damaged the chair?

Checklist

- A verb is a time–action word: *ran, complained, was sleeping*.
- A noun is a label for a person, place or thing: *child, button, park*.
- The same word can be either a noun or a verb depending on how it is used in a sentence.

Key idea 3: Adjectives

Adjectives tell us more about nouns – they help us paint a clearer picture of a noun. At school I was taught they were 'describing' words – they add to or describe the meaning of a noun. So let's see how they add to or describe nouns.

Picture a table in your mind's eye. What can you tell me about the table you see? Is it *wooden* or *plastic*? Is it *modern* or *antique*? Is it *round*, *square* or *oval*, *smooth* or *rough*, *attractive*, *beautiful* or *ugly*, a *dining* table or a *kitchen* table?

All of the words you can use to describe the table are adjectives and their purpose is to tell us more about a person or a thing. Without them, every table is just a table.

Notice that an adjective may come either before or after the noun it describes. We can say *The table is wooden* or we can talk about *the wooden table*; we can say *The table is blue* or we can talk about *the blue table*.

Now look at these nouns and try to think of some adjectives that might be used to give more information about each of them:

wine
doughnuts
teapot
news

Here are some suggestions I thought of for each one – you may not have chosen the same adjectives:

wine
red, white, sparkling, rosé, expensive, delicious ...
doughnuts
ring, jam, chocolate, fattening, unhealthy ...
teapot
china, chipped, stainless steel, empty, green ...
news
hot, depressing, fascinating, bad, good ...

Adjectives need nouns!

You can't use adjectives on their own. Your readers or listeners must know which noun each adjective you use goes with. For example, the word *beautiful* is an adjective, but we can only understand this if we have been told *who* or *what* is beautiful.

a *beautiful* painting
a *beautiful* view
a *beautiful* model

How to find an adjective in a sentence

To find which words in a sentence are adjectives, the first thing you need to do is to identify the noun or nouns. Then look for any word or words that tell you more about the nouns. Remember they could be before or after the noun.

Let's look at a sentence:

This book I'm reading is brilliant.

Ask yourself what is the noun – a label for a person, thing or place. The answer is *book*. Now look for a word that tells you more about the book. The word *brilliant* tells us what sort of book it is, and *brilliant* is an adjective.

Quick check

Mask the answers and underline the adjectives. What noun does each adjective describe? Unmask the text and check your answers.

1 The hot sun burnt their fair skin.
hot (describing *sun*), fair (describing *skin*)

2 The sea was cool.
cool (describing *sea*)

3 The meal was expensive considering how cheap the ingredients were.
expensive (describing *meal*), cheap (describing *ingredients*)

4 The stormy weather has brought severe flooding to coastal areas.
stormy (describing *weather*), severe (describing *flooding*), coastal (describing *areas*)

5 His charming manner landed him a superb job.
charming (describing *manner*), superb (describing *job*)

Now really test yourself

Underline all the adjectives in the following sentences. Check your answers on page 205.

1 They asked for the most expensive main course.

2 The successful shop closed and moved to the new shopping centre.

3 Eat plenty of green vegetables.

4 She was invited to attend the jazz concert.

5 The secondary school announced its new policy on absenteeism.

6 The delayed start of the film meant many people had to leave early.

7 She chose a cotton blouse and a green silk skirt.

8 The recent announcement has caused uncertainty.

9 An estate car drew up outside the semi-detached house.

10 Air travel creates high levels of pollution.

Checklist

- Adjectives give us more detail about a noun. By using adjectives we can paint a clearer picture of what we mean. We can describe the noun *landscape* by using adjectives such as *rolling, hilly* or *mountainous; stunning, treacherous* or *ugly*.
- Adjectives can come before or after a noun: *the* ***beautiful*** *landscape; the landscape is* ***beautiful***.
- Adjectives don't have a meaning on their own, but make sense when we know what noun they are describing.

Key idea 4: Adverbs

As the name suggests, adverbs tell us more about verbs. They tell us *how*, *how often*, *where* or *when* something happens, has happened or will happen.

Let's look at some sentences that have adverbs:

They drank *slowly*.
John *never* reads the paper.
She arrived *today*.
They'll live *here*.

In the first sentence, *slowly* is an adverb. It tells us *how* they drank. In the other sentences, the words *never*, *today* and *here* are adverbs. These words answer the questions *how often?*, *when?* and *where?*

How to find an adverb in a sentence

To find which words in a sentence are adverbs, the first step is to identify the verb or verbs. Then look for any word or words that tell you more about how, how often, when or where the action of the verb happens.

Let's look at a sentence:

They ate slowly.

Ask yourself what is the verb – the time–action word. The answer is *ate*. Now look for a word that tells you more about how, how often, where or when they ate. The word *slowly* tells us *how* they ate, and *slowly* is an adverb.

Tip: You can often recognize adverbs by the fact that they end in the letters *-ly*. For example, *quickly*, *easily* and *softly* are all adverbs.

Adverbs can often be several words

In the sentences we have looked at so far, the adverb has been a single word. However, often a group of words, or a *phrase*, does the job of an adverb. Look at these examples:

They laughed *in an insincere way*.
They arrived *before the rain*.
They'll move to Spain *after the wedding*.

The phrases in italics all tell us more about verbs: *in an insincere way* tells us *how* they laughed; *before the rain* tells us *when* they arrived; *after the wedding* tells us *when* they'll move.

Quick check

Mask the answers. Find the verbs in each sentence and then underline any adverbs that go with them. Unmask the text and check your answers.

1 They laughed helplessly.

helplessly (describes how they *laughed*)

2 The team played brilliantly.

brilliantly (describes how the team *played*)

3 The bird soared effortlessly.

effortlessly (describes how the bird *soared*)

4 The pound rose rapidly against the euro

rapidly (describes how the pound *rose*)

5 They met for lunch later.

later (describes when they *met*)

6 They never eat apples.

never (describes how often they *eat* apples)

Mask the answers and underline the adverbs. Unmask the text and check your answers.

1 At the end of the evening he wrote the letter carefully.

at the end of the evening, carefully

2 On 15 March 2002, they triumphantly signed the treaty.

on 15 March 2002, triumphantly

3 He invited us into the hall in a formal manner.

in a formal manner

4 She wanted to finish the project before the summer was over.

before the summer was over

5 Before the match started the teams eyed each other warily.

before the match started, warily

6 The boy fell badly and screamed at the top of his voice.

badly, at the top of his voice

Now really test yourself

Underline all the adverbs in the following sentences. Check your answers on pages 205–6.

1 They usually get up around 7 o'clock.

2 Emily slept soundly.

3 She couldn't run quickly because her back was bad.

4 The policemen checked the evidence thoroughly.

5 The man played well and won convincingly.

6 The teachers nodded encouragingly at the end of the performance.

7 The course ended disastrously – no one passed the exam!

8 Why doesn't he try hard?

9 His book was widely read.

10 Sarah spoke to me boldly about her plans.

11 They packed their bags at top speed.

12 Nick played endlessly on the computer.

13 Alex worked on his project in his bedroom with enthusiasm.

14 They voted for Jones unanimously.

15 He criticized their work mercilessly.

Checklist

- An adverb is a word that tells us more about *how*, *how often*, *where* or *when* an action takes place: *never, at 6pm, slowly, embarrassingly, in Trafalgar Square*.
- Adverbs often end in *-ly*: *quickly, strangely*.
- Adverbs can be a single word (*well, happily, now*) or be a phrase (*at the end of the evening, before next summer, on the edge of the cliff*).

Adverbs and adjectives

You now know the difference between adverbs and adjectives:

- adjectives go with nouns
- adverbs go with verbs

It's a common mistake in written English to put an adverb with a noun, or an adjective with a verb.

× He walks good.

The word *good* is an adjective, and so it should go with a noun. It does not go with the word *walks*, which is a verb.

✓ He walks well.

The word *well* is an adverb, and this does go with the verb *walks*.

Quick check

Mask the answers and pick out the adjectives and the adverbs in each sentence. Remember to look for nouns and verbs. Are there any words that tell you more about each noun? These words are adjectives. Are there any words or phrases that tell you more about the verb? These are adverbs. Unmask the text and check your answers.

1 He marched rapidly away from the ignited fuse.
adjective: ignited; adverb: rapidly

2 They couldn't agree completely on a solution.
adverb: completely

3 He forcefully elbowed his way into the packed room.
adjective: packed; adverb: forcefully

4 The governors must carefully weigh up the long-term implications of the school's involvement.
adjective: long-term; adverb: carefully

5 Joe didn't allow the dramatic scenery to stop him driving properly.
adjective: dramatic; adverb: properly

6 Lisa played the sax beautifully until she was rudely interrupted by her brother.
adverbs: beautifully, rudely

Now really test yourself

Underline all the adjectives and adverbs in the following sentences. Check your answers on page 206.

1 John refused to eat the dried-up sandwiches.

2 The new keeper performed magnificently.

3 The river flowed rapidly though the spectacular gorges.

4 The chef instantly produced a delicious meal for the grateful travellers.

5 The tomatoes ripened gradually in the wet summer.

6 No amount of practice will help him play that violin well.

7 The beach filled up rapidly with excited children and their families.

8 Why don't we use renewable energy sources whenever possible?

In which of these sentences are adverbs and adjectives used incorrectly? Check your answers on page 206.

1 He walked home quick.

2 They ran too slow to catch the crowded bus.

3 Why did he do the job so bad?

4 How did they manage to complete the course successfully?

5 Was the course successful?

6 They wrote the letter neat.

Checklist

- An adjective is a word that tells you more about a noun: *a* ***new*** *report; the* ***latest*** *idea; a* ***beautiful*** *sunset*.
- An adverb is a word that tells you more about a verb – how, where or when something was done: *he drank* ***quickly****; they arrived* ***at 10pm****; they announced the cuts* ***in Birmingham***.

Key idea 5: Subjects and objects

What does *subject* mean?

In everyday language the word *subject* means 'what something's about'; but when we describe language, the word *subject* has a specific meaning.

The subject of a verb is a person or thing that comes in front of the verb and controls the verb. It is usually (but not always) the person or thing doing the action described by the verb.

sentence	***subject***	***verb***
He ate the sandwich.	he	ate
The manager put together a plan.	the manager	put together
The girls finished their homework.	the girls	finished
John and Jim asked for some food.	John and Jim	asked for
Alex gave a CD to Nick.	Alex	gave
The letters were sent last week.	the letters	were sent

Quick check

Mask the answers. Pick out the subject and verb in each sentence. Unmask the text and check your answers.

1 I wrote the letter last night.

wrote = verb; I = subject

2 Daisy takes Tamsin to the cinema every week.

takes = verb; Daisy = subject

3 The bird is watching the fish in the river.

is watching = verb; the bird = subject

4 We corresponded for 10 years.

corresponded = verb; we = subject

5 Jack and Jill went up the hill.

went up = verb; Jack and Jill = subject

6 They live in Switzerland.

live = verb; they = subject

What does *object* mean?

When we describe language, the word *object* has a specific meaning. While the subject represents the person or thing that does the action, the object represents *the person or thing in a sentence having something done to it*.

We've already seen that the subject comes *before* a verb. Objects usually come *after* the verb.

sentence	***verb***	***object***
He read the book.	read	the book (the thing he read)
They liked chocolate.	liked	chocolate (the thing they liked)
Nick helped him.	helped	him (the person Nick helped)
Don't eat this.	eat	this (the thing you must not eat)

The examples also show the most common word order in English: first **subject**, then **verb**, and last **object**.

Quick check

Mask the answers. Pick out the object in each sentence. Unmask the text and check your answers.

1 John ignored the advice.

advice

2 She peeled the onions.

onions

3 Nick saw Cora at the station.

Cora

4 They opened the map.

map

5 She wrapped the present.

present

6 The report outlined the crisis in Africa.

crisis

7 Alex met Nick and Edward at the library.

Nick and Edward

More about objects

A sentence does not have to have an object. Take a look at these examples. There are no objects in these sentences:

They ate at 7pm.
He ran.
They jumped.
She giggled.
They got dressed and then they set off.

No object is required here because the action described by the verb is complete in itself.

On the other hand, some sentences have more than one object.

I gave him the book.
They offered her the chance to study in France.

In the first sentence, *him* and *the book* are both objects of *gave*. In the second sentence, *her* and *the chance* are both objects of *offered*.

Now really test yourself

Underline the subjects and objects in the following sentences. Check your answers on page 207.

1 The book described her journey to China.

2 Flowers brighten up a room.

3 The teacher announced the plan for the term.

4 Chocolate cake helps concentration.

5 He took the wrong road and arrived late.

6 I can't help you.

7 Solar panels reduce electricity consumption.

8 Weeds grow quickly in warm weather.

Checklist

- The subject of a sentence is the person or thing that comes before the verb and controls the verb: ***he*** *likes cheese;* ***I*** *like chocolate*.
- The subject of a sentence is not necessarily the person or thing doing the action described by the verb: ***the man*** *was bitten by the dog*.
- The object of a sentence is the person or thing having the action done to it. It usually comes after the verb: *he's mending* ***my bike***; *they met* ***their friends*** *yesterday*.
- Not every sentence needs to have an object.

Key idea 6: Using the right form of the verb

Now you know what subjects and verbs are, let's look at the special relationship between them. We can see this in English especially when we talk about the present time.

Let's look at some sentences using the verb *arrive*.

We say:

I arrive.
you arrive.
we arrive.
they arrive.

But we say:

He arrive**s**.
She arrive**s**.
It arrive**s**.

What is going on here is that the subjects control the form of the verb: if *he*, *she* or *it* is the subject, the verb needs an *-s* added. This is called **agreement**. We can say that the form of the verb must **agree** with the subject of the verb.

Let's look at an example:

× She arrive after me.

Arrive is the wrong form to use here because the verb must agree with the subject *she*. To make the verb agree with *she*, we must change *arrive* to *arrive***s**:

✓ She arrives after me.

What we've done is make the verb – *arrives* – agree with the subject – *she* – so the sentence is now grammatically correct.

Here's another example:

× They usually arrives after me.

Arrives is the wrong form to use here because the verb must agree with the subject *they*. To make the verb agree with *they*, we must change *arrives* to *arrive*:

✓ They usually arrive after me.

Quick check

Mask the answers. Check whether the subject and verb agree in these sentences. Unmask the text and check your answers.

1 They hates a fuss.
incorrect (they hate)

2 He loves coffee.
correct

3 She run to school every day.
incorrect (she runs)

4 We wants fresh fish for supper.
incorrect (we want)

5 They drive on the left-hand side of the road in Japan.
correct

6 It gives off an unpleasant smell when attacked.
correct

Subject–verb agreement in questions

Let's look at how the idea of agreement applies to some other types of sentence.

We say:

Do I arrive?
Do you arrive?
Do we arrive?
Do they arrive?

But we say:

Does he arrive?
Does she arrive?
Does it arrive?

When we ask a question, we still need an *-s* for the subjects *he*, *she* and *it*, but the *-s* appears in the word *does*.

Subject–verb agreement in negatives

The same thing happens when we make negative statements.

We say:

I don't arrive.
You don't arrive.
We don't arrive.
They don't arrive.

But we say:

He **doesn't** arrive.
She **doesn't** arrive.
It **doesn't** arrive.

Quick check

Mask the answers. Check whether the subject and verb agree in these sentences. Unmask the text and check your answers.

1 Does they like sandwiches?
incorrect (do they like)

2 We don't want frozen vegetables.
correct

3 He doesn't want coffee.
correct

4 Doesn't you live in Luton?
incorrect (don't you live)

5 Do she run home every day?
incorrect (does she run)

6 Do you need more time?
correct

7 Doesn't I look good in this?
incorrect (don't I look)

8 Does they drive on the right-hand side of the road in France?
incorrect (do they drive)

Subject–verb agreement with other subjects

The subject of the verb can be the name of a person, place or thing as well as a word like *I*, *you*, *he* or *she*. The principle of agreement still applies.

Alex and Nick usually arrive after me.

Alex and Nick could be represented by *they*, but not by *he*. So the form of the verb must be the one that agrees with *they*. That is *arrive*.

But the form of the verb is different if we only talk about one person.

Alex usually arrives after me.

Alex could be represented by *he*, but not by *they*. So the form of the verb must be the one that agrees with *he*. That is *arrives* – not *arrive*.

Quick check

Mask the answers. Which word could you use to replace the subject in each sentence? Unmask the text and check your answers.

1 Anita only drinks coffee.
she

2 Wanda and I have lunch together every Thursday.
we

3 Tommy and Karl opened the shop in 1990.
they

4 Anna and the salesman argued about the price.
they

5 My sister has got a new Ferrari.
she

6 You and I both know that's not true.
we

Subject–verb agreement and the verb *be*

Making the subject and verb agree can sometimes involve more than just deciding whether or not to add an *-s*.

Let's look at some sentences that use the verb *be*.

We say:

I *am* delighted.
You *are* easy-going.
We *are* tired.
They *are* determined.
The boys (= they) *are* determined.
Alison (= she) *is* naughty.

Notice that *am*, *are* and *is* are all different forms of *be*. The correct form to use depends on the subject of the verb.

Ask yourself if the next example is right or wrong, then ask yourself why:

I is happy.

I is the subject and the form that agrees with *I* is *am* (not *is*).

✓ I am happy.

Now let's look at the forms of the verb *be* that are used to talk about the past.

I was
he was
she was
it was
we were
you were
they were

Ask yourself if the next example is right or wrong, then ask yourself why:

Pete were happy.

Pete (= *he*) is the subject and the form that agrees with *he* is *was* (not *were*).

✓ Pete was happy.

It is quite a common mistake to use *was* after *we*, *you* and *they*. But you wouldn't fall into that trap, would you?

Quick check

Mask the answers. Check whether the subject and verb agree in these sentences. Unmask the text and check your answers.

1 He were late home last night.
incorrect (he was)

2 They wasn't allowed any help.
incorrect (they weren't)

3 They were delighted with the report.
correct

4 The allotment was in a terrible state.
correct

5 The disasters was caused by the heavy rain.
incorrect (they were)

Subject–verb agreement and the verb *have*

Another common verb that has some slightly unusual forms is *have*.

When talking about the present, we say:

I have
you have
we have
they have

But we say:

he **has**
she **has**
it **has**

And when talking about the past, the form *had* agrees with whatever subject you use.

I had	he had
you had	she had
we had	it had
they had	

Quick check

Mask the answers. Check whether the subject and verb agree in these sentences. Unmask the text and check your answers.

1 The reports were completed early.
correct (they were)

2 The girls have decided to have fish instead of meat.
correct (they have)

3 Many children don't like doing homework.
correct (they don't)

4 I tells you everything.
incorrect (I tell)

5 The law protect them.
incorrect (it protects)

Invisible subject–verb agreement

In many sentences we can't see subject–verb agreement, particularly when we talk about the future or the past.

For example:

He protected them.
They protected them.

These sentences have different subjects, but the form of the verb – *protected* – stays the same. The principle that the subject controls the verb still holds true. But in this case the form of the verb required by the different subjects just happens to be the same.

The same is true in this example:

The boy will not like the new regime.
The boys will not like the new regime.

Now really test yourself

Do the subjects and verbs agree in these sentences? Check your answers on pages 207–8.

1 I wants a new toy.

2 He wants a new pencil.

3 They wanted to go home.

4 John decide how to run the company.

5 He don't want to employ unqualified staff.

6 They don't want to work for him.

7 Do he have to take on qualified staff?

8 Do they have to do what he tells them?

9 Ann and Mike has taken the decision to close the factory.

10 The laws is there to protect us all.

11 He don't have any ink left.

12 Sally and Joe hasn't bought the shopping.

13 We wasn't late for the meeting.

14 They don't have any cheese left.

15 The children hasn't done their homework.

16 The sandwiches tastes horrible.

17 Chocolates is bad for your teeth.

18 He takes too many people in his car.

19 I were shocked at the news.

20 Why isn't they here?

Using the right form when writing about the past

Before we leave the topic of verbs, we need to look at another problem that people can have when choosing which form of the verb to use.

Take a look at these two sentences:

- × I have wrote this letter to answer your queries.
- ✓ I have written this letter to answer your queries.

Can you see why the first sentence is wrong?

How about these?

- ✓ He has come home early.
- × He has came home early.

Can you see why the second sentence is wrong?

If you recognize that instantly then there is no need to read on. But carry on if you are not sure …

What is the problem?

There are different ways of writing about past time. We can use just one word for the verb:

I *wrote* a letter.
He *came* home early.

Or we can use *have* or *has* with a form of the verb:

I *have written* a letter.
He *has come* home early.

For most verbs the same form is used in both cases, so there is not a problem:

I *walked*.	I *have walked*.
They *finished*.	They *have finished*.
He *decided*.	He *has decided*.

But for a few common verbs, there are **two different forms**: one that you use on its own, and one that you use after *have* or *has*.

A list of difficult verbs

Look at the list below. This shows verbs that have two different forms for writing about the past. Test yourself by covering one of the columns and seeing if you can tell the other form of the verb:

I ate	I have eaten
I began	I have begun
I blew	I have blown
I came	I have come
I drank	I have drunk
I lay down	I have lain down
I mowed	I have mown
I ran	I have run
I sang	I have sung
I saw	I have seen
I spoke	I have spoken
I swam	I have swum
I took	I have taken
I undid	I have undone
I was	I have been
I went	I have gone
I wrote	I have written

Quick check

Mask the answers. Is the verb in the right form? Correct any that are wrong. Unmask the text and check your answers.

1 They have begun their walk.

correct

2 The director hasn't spoke yet.

incorrect (he hasn't spoken)

3 They blew bubbles.

correct

4 He has swam to the island.

incorrect (he has swum)

5 They gone home about midnight.

incorrect (they went)

Now really test yourself

Correct any verbs that are in the wrong form. Check your answers on page 208.

1 John spoke about the new book.

2 He done it yesterday.

3 What has he drank?

4 They have wrote about everything they done.

5 My ankle's swelled up horribly after the fall.

6 They eaten before they left.

7 Has he ate yet?

8 He has laid down.

9 She lied down on the sofa.

10 I drunk too many glasses of water.

11 Why has he went there?

12 Has the manager spoken to you yet?

13 They swum out beyond the coral reef.

14 Has he mowed the garden yet?

15 They haven't taken anything away.

Checklist

- The subject controls the form of the verb. This is most obvious in the present tense: ***I like*** *apples;* ***she likes*** *pears.*
- To make sure you have used the correct form of the verb, check the subject and the verb, and make sure that they go together.
- Some verbs have only one form for talking about the past, but some have two different forms.
- Watch out for verbs that have two forms to talk about the past. Make sure you use the right form of the verb: *I ate; I have eaten; he ran; he has run.*

Key idea 7: Pronouns

A pronoun is a word we can use instead of a noun. The words *I*, *you*, *he*, *she*, *it*, *we*, *they*, *me*, *him*, *her*, *us*, *them*, *this* and *that* are all pronouns.

The following sentence has the noun *Peter* as its subject:

> Peter found a stamp.

The sentence will still work if we use the pronoun *he* to replace *Peter*:

> He found a stamp.

Why do we need pronouns?

This is what happens if we avoid using pronouns:

> Peter finished the letters. Peter then put the letters in an envelope. Peter found a stamp and stuck the stamp on the envelope. Then Peter went to the letterbox to put his letter into the letterbox.

Repeating *Peter*, *letter*, *stamp*, *letterbox* a number of times in a sentence – whether we're writing or speaking – is likely to get boring for readers or listeners.

Instead of repeating *Peter*, we can write *he*. *He* is a pronoun that replaces the noun *Peter*.

So what pronouns could you use for *letters*, *stamp*, *letterbox* and *envelope*?

Instead of repeating *stamp*, *letterbox* and *envelope* we can write *it*; instead of repeating *letters* we can write *them*.

Notice that we replace the plural word *letters* with *them*, but the singular words with *he* or *it*.

If we use pronouns we can write:

> Peter finished the letters. He then put them in an envelope. He found a stamp and stuck it on the envelope. Then he went to the letterbox to put his letter into it.

I hope you'll agree that this is a much more natural-sounding paragraph.

Quick check

Mask the answers and pick out the pronouns in each sentence. Unmask the text and check your answers.

1 She didn't like potatoes.

she

2 They hadn't time to finish it.

they, it

3 It was late and we couldn't find them.

it, we, them

4 I wanted to go to France.

I

5 Do you like it?

you, it

6 Why don't we do that?

we, that

7 Can you help me with this?

you, me, this

What can go wrong with pronouns?

A quick glance back at the exercise above should show you one possible problem with pronouns. If we don't know what *it*, *him*, *them* or *this* refers to, we can't understand what is meant. As ever, if we're speaking we'll soon realize people haven't followed us, but in writing we only get one chance.

When you look back over something you have written, check that each pronoun you've used clearly refers to a noun that you have already used. That way the person who's reading can understand what you mean.

Choose the right pronoun for the noun you are replacing

The pronoun you use must match the person or thing that it stands for. Not only that, but you may need to use a different pronoun depending on whether the word you are replacing is the subject (see page 36) or the object (see page 37) of the verb.

Look at this sentence:

Alex helped Nick.

Alex is the subject and *Nick* is the object. If we want to replace *Alex* with a pronoun, we need to use the pronoun for the subject, but if we want to replace *Nick* with a pronoun, we need to use a different pronoun:

He helped Nick.
Alex helped *him*.

Here is a basic table of pronouns:

	subject pronoun	***object pronoun***
For something masculine, eg *boy* or *man*	he	him
For something feminine, eg *girl* or *woman*	she	her
For things that are not human, eg *tree*	it	it
For all plurals, eg *boys*, *trees* or *women*	they	them
For the person who is writing or speaking	I	me
For the person or people they are writing or speaking to	you	you
For the person who is writing or speaking and other people too	we	us

Remember that **subjects** come before the verb and control it, while **objects** indicate the person or thing having something done to them.

Quick check

Mask the answers. Pick out any subject and object pronouns in these sentences. Unmask the text and check your answers.

1 Peter gave Sophie and Tamsin a book. They were very surprised.
they (subject pronoun)

2 The teacher told the pupils off and she gave them a detention.
she (subject pronoun), them (object pronoun)

3 If you've decided to paint the house – why not paint it red?
you (subject pronoun), it (object pronoun)

4 The reports were published on Tuesday – but they are too long.
they (subject pronoun)

5 I don't think many people will read them.
I (subject pronoun), them (object pronoun)

6 Vadik told me he intended to retire.
me (object pronoun), he (subject pronoun)

7 Renata invited us to the concert.
us (object pronoun)

8 The cup slipped off the tray. It broke into tiny pieces.
it (subject pronoun)

9 Ask her why she didn't turn up.
her (object pronoun), she (subject pronoun)

10 They invited us for dinner.
they (subject pronoun), us (object pronoun)

11 I've read it at least ten times.
I (subject pronoun), it (object pronoun)

12 The plants thrived after you watered them.
you (subject pronoun), them (object pronoun)

Some related words

While we are looking at pronouns, I will mention two other groups of words.

First are words used as adjectives when we are talking about who something belongs to. (These are called 'possessive adjectives').

For example:

Here are *my* cousins.
Where are *your* slippers?
Where's *their* house?

We can fit this group of words into the table we've just looked at:

subject pronoun	***object pronoun***	***possessive adjective***
he	him	his
she	her	her
it	it	its
they	them	their
I	me	my
you	you	your
we	us	our

Second are words called 'possessive pronouns'. These replace a noun and a possessive adjective, so *her towel* becomes *hers* and *their house* becomes *theirs*:

My towel is green. *Hers* is pink.
Our house is tiny compared with *theirs*.

We can add this group of words to make a fourth column on our table:

subject pronoun	***object pronoun***	***possessive adjective***	***possessive pronoun***
he	him	his	his
she	her	her	hers
it	it	its	its
they	them	their	theirs
I	me	my	mine
you	you	your	yours
we	us	our	ours

An important thing to notice about the words in this column is that none is spelt with an apostrophe.

Confusion of *he, she* and *it*

Sometimes it can be tricky to decide which pronoun to use. Look at these two sentences:

The dog ran up to the girl – it jumped up and wagged its tail.
The dog ran up to the girl – he jumped up and wagged his tail.

Which is correct? It depends on how much of an animal lover you are as to whether you call a dog *he* or *it*. But you'll need to be consistent. Decide if the dog is *he*, *she* or *it* and stick to that.

How about the next example? Could there be any misunderstandings?

The dog ran up to the girl – she jumped up and wagged its tail.

The pronoun *she* could be confusing. Does it refer to the girl or the dog? If we are using *its* to refer to the dog, then the reader will expect that *she* refers to the girl. And that leaves us with a rather odd scene.

Quick check

Mask the answers. Pick out the pronouns and say what they refer to. Which ones might be confusing? Unmask the text and check your answers.

1 The dogs ran into the road. They braked suddenly to avoid hitting them.
they = the people in the car
(there is a possible confusion as we might imagine the dogs braked),
them = the dogs

2 The cat purred happily on the sofa. She was in seventh heaven.
she = the cat

3 In the restaurant James and Sarah ate elaborate ice creams. They looked wonderful.
they = ice creams or James and Sarah
(there is a possible confusion as either might look wonderful)

4 The concert ended suddenly. It had not gone well from the start.
it = the concert

5 The doctor called the next patient in. She had been working all day and looked very tired.
she = the doctor or the patient
(there is a possible confusion as either might look tired)

Confusion of *it* and *they*

Think about the word *government*. Is it singular or plural? Would you refer to a government as *it* or *they*?

Look at these two sentences and decide which you would say:

The government says it is putting more money into the NHS.
The government say they are putting more money into the NHS.

Technically *government* is a singular noun so the first sentence is correct. But people often use *government* as a plural because it is made up of many people. So both sentences could be considered correct. If we use *they* and plural verbs, our writing sounds more everyday – more fluent. If we use *it* and singular verbs, our writing sounds more formal.

It doesn't really matter which you choose, but the key thing is to be consistent. Once you have chosen *it* for the government you must stick to that, and make all your verbs agree with *it* (see page 40).

Quick check

Mask the answers. Are these passages consistent? Check the subject, any subject pronouns and the verbs. Do they all agree? Unmask the text and check your answers.

1 Sainsbury's has cut their prices.
inconsistent (has = singular; their = plural)

2 BT have changed its pricing policy.
inconsistent (have = plural; its = singular)

3 The baker's has decided to stop selling their delicious wholemeal rolls.
inconsistent (has = singular; their = plural)

4 The school have announced significant changes to the uniform. They want the children to wear green shirts rather than blue ones.
consistent (have = plural; they = plural)

5 The local post office has said it won't be able to stay open much longer.
consistent (has = singular; it = singular)

Remember: When writing about an organization, decide if you want to treat it as *it* or *they*, and stick to your decision. Check your verbs too!

Confusion of *I* and *me*

The words *I* and *me* are both pronouns. They both refer to the person who's speaking or writing. But they are not the same. They should not be used in the same places. But they often are.

So what's the difference between them? Think back to the difference between the *subject* and the *object*. (See pages 36–7 if you need to remind yourself.) The difference between *I* and *me* is that *I* is the subject pronoun and *me* is the object pronoun.

So *I* needs to go in front of the verb and control the verb:

> *I* met the new teacher last week.
> *I* chose the new secretary from 20 applicants.

And *me* needs to be used for the object – the person having something done to them. It comes after the verb:

> The new teacher met *me*.
> The secretary chose *me* to help her.

This probably sounds rather obvious in these examples. It gets slightly more tricky when there are other people involved in the sentence. Let's look at some harder examples:

- × The manager and me went to the meeting.
- ✓ He and I couldn't agree what to do.
- × She wanted her brother and I to help her.

The best way to deal with these – and know you are right – is to get rid of the other people in the sentence, just temporarily. Let's look at the first example again:

- × The manager and me went to the meeting.

If we remove *the manager* we get:

> [...] me went to the meeting.

This probably sounds wrong to you. We need the subject pronoun *I* in front of the verb *went*:

- ✓ I went to the meeting.
- ✓ The manager and I went to the meeting.

> **Tip:** When deciding if you need *I* or *me*, remove the other people from the sentence.

Quick check

Mask the answers. Look at how the pronouns are used in these sentences. Say if they're right or wrong and correct them if they're wrong. Unmask the text and check your answers.

1 My friend and I went for a walk this morning.
correct (I went)

2 Sarah and me invited Jane to the party.
incorrect (I invited)

3 The presenters asked Bart and me to appear in the programme.
correct (asked me)

4 Alex and Ellis invited Louise and I to their dress rehearsal.
incorrect (invited me)

5 Nick wanted Patrick, Flora and me to see the film with him.
correct (wanted me)

6 Suzanne, Cathy and me had a relaxing time at the pool.
incorrect (I had)

7 Why can't Chris and I meet you later?
correct (I meet)

8 Please don't ask Anne or I to help with the dinner.
incorrect (ask me)

9 They teased the students and I.
incorrect (teased me)

10 Zoë couldn't decide whether to play cricket with Alice and me.
correct (play cricket with me)

Now really test yourself

Look at how the pronouns are used in these sentences. Say if they're right or wrong and correct them if they're wrong. Check your answers on page 209.

1 The cat wanted to come in, so they banged their nose on the window.

2 They told Jack and I to send our applications in immediately.

3 The mobile phone company has put up its prices.

4 The manager and I have asked for the complaint to be investigated.

5 The police told my manager and I they had already looked into the problem.

6 The government has asked us all to look at their policies on health and education.

7 The parrot was rather talkative so I gave it a sunflower seed. I can't repeat what he said in reply!

8 Jane and me would like to come to the party on Friday.

Checklist

- Pronouns are words that can replace nouns.
- Some are used to replace subjects (*I, you, he, she, it, we, they*) and some to replace objects (*me, you, him, her, us, them*). Make sure you choose the right pronoun to replace the noun.
- Make sure your reader will know who or what is referred to by the pronoun you have chosen.
- Be careful when choosing between *I* and *me*, between *it* and *they*, and between *it* and *he* or *she*.

Key idea 8: Complete sentences

We need to write in sentences to help our readers. When our readers see a full stop they can pause to check they've understood what we've written.

At school I was taught that a sentence begins with a capital letter and ends with a full stop. But just using a capital letter and a full stop doesn't necessarily mean that a sentence is complete and that it will make sense to our readers.

Look at this sentence:

× The man likes.

This example begins with a capital letter and ends with a full stop, but it is not complete, and it does not help our readers.

Sentences should contain a single complete idea.

The parts of a sentence

Before we can go further we need to be clear about what makes a sentence. Look at these examples:

✓ I read.
× The man likes.

Both examples contain a subject and a verb, but the first example makes a complete sentence, while the second does not.

So why isn't the second example a sentence?

The difference is that the verb *like* needs an object to complete the sense, whereas *read* can have an object but doesn't have to have one. What would you need to do to turn the second example into a sentence? It's missing something. If we add a noun – the thing the man likes – it becomes a sentence that we recognize is complete:

✓ The man likes chocolate.

So it looks as if to make a sentence we always need a subject and a verb, and we sometimes also need an object. We might express this as a formula:

subject + verb (+ object)

Let's test our theory:

✓ I read the book.

This includes a subject (*I*), a verb (*read*) and an object (*the book*).

Incomplete sentences

How about this? Is it a complete sentence?

× As I was reading my book.

This includes a subject (*I*) a verb (*was reading*) and an object (*my book*). But you can probably sense that it is missing something. It does not express a complete idea to the reader.

The problem lies with the little word *as*. This word suggests to the reader that what follows is the less important part of the sentence, and that the main idea will come later.

How could we turn it into a sentence? There are two ways:

- Add a main idea so that it makes complete sense:

  As I was reading my book, I heard the door open.

- Remove the word *as*, the word that is telling us this phrase is the less important part of the sentence:

  I was reading my book.

These are two different approaches but both have enabled us to make complete sense.

Let's look at another example:

× While they waited.

This is not a complete sentence. It's incomplete because of the word *while*. Again, we can either add a main idea to complete the sense, or we can remove *while*, the word that is making this phrase less important:

✓ While they waited, the repairer fixed the heels on her shoes.
✓ They waited.

Quick check

Mask the answers. Are these complete sentences? Unmask the text and check your answers.

1 She announced their engagement.
complete

2 The long list of books on the shelf.
incomplete (it needs a verb)

3 Although they liked her.
incomplete (because of the word *although*)

4 The council reviewed its policy on street traders.
complete

5 Guarded the front door.
incomplete (it needs a subject)

6 Fahad invited.
incomplete (*invited* needs an object)

7 Letters were sent to the parents of all pupils.
complete

8 While Lynne was running to the gym.
incomplete (because of the word *while*)

9 Following the recent rise in petrol prices.
incomplete (because of the word *following*)

10 Chris decided to rent a small office.
complete

Now really test yourself

Say whether these are complete sentences. Correct them if they're not. Check your answers on pages 209–10.

1 Claire and Annie passed their exams with flying colours.

2 Helen spending a year in Canada.

3 Charles flew to South America with.

4 Cathy preparing for her next trip to France.

5 While the documents were being prepared.

6 With reference to your recent letter.

7 Decided to borrow the book instead.

8 The managers, with a great reputation for getting things sorted.

9 The few remaining members of the football team.

10 Decisions were being slowly.

Checklist

- A sentence needs a subject and a verb.
- Some sentences also need an object to complete the sense of the verb.
- A sentence needs to make complete sense in itself.

PART B
GOOD PUNCTUATION

Your readers deserve good punctuation

After you've spent time planning and writing something, and then more time checking over it, it would be sad to lose your readers because of poor punctuation.

But without good punctuation, your readers may need to spend too long looking at what you have written – re-reading it, re-grouping the words, trying to work out how to read it and what it means.

Good punctuation can be the difference between reading something once and understanding it straight away and having to read it two or three times but still being unsure of what is meant. How many readers have that much time on their hands?

Good punctuation is invisible to the reader. It's there to help us read and understand the first time we read something. We probably notice it only when there's something wrong with it – usually when there's too much of it … or else too little.

What's right and what's wrong?

Punctuation is not like spelling – it's not something you can check in the dictionary. You can check whether to write *recieve* or *receive* pretty quickly and with 100% confidence. There are some uses of punctuation that are definitely wrong and would confuse your reader, but there may be several different – and equally correct – ways to punctuate the same piece of writing.

> **Tip:** A golden rule of punctuation is to use it sparingly: if in doubt, leave it out.

What can you get out of this section of the book?

This part of the book will:

- explain how the most important marks of punctuation are used
- give examples of each
- point out the most common errors
- let you practise until you're confident you can punctuate well

Key idea 1: Full stops

Full stops separate sentences. They give the reader a place to pause and make sense of the words in the previous sentence.

If you can get full stops in the right places and use enough of them in your writing, you'll also make the rest of the job of adding punctuation easier for yourself.

Not enough full stops?

If sentences are too long we struggle to remember the words we've read and to see how the words fit together and make sense. Without enough full stops, reading can become a strain. Our eyes may start to jump along the line, not really reading what's there because the going is too tough.

A good average sentence length is 15–20 words and a sentence should cover one idea. So when you first plan and write your letter or e-mail, focus on keeping your sentences to a reasonable length.

Too many full stops?

It's worth keeping in mind that lots of five- or six-word sentences, one after another, make for a rather boring read.

Sentences don't have to be of any fixed length. The following sentences are of varying length, but none of them is any more correct than the others:

> They wanted to have enough volunteers to complete the work in a weekend.
> She asked me to return the books I had borrowed.
> The children left home early.
> Ann's gone to bed.

Quick check

Read this short paragraph and divide it into sentences using full stops. Check your answer over the page.

> The boys and girls had decided on a day out at the beach to celebrate the beginning of term the weather forecast was brilliant and the blue skies early on confirmed that it was going to be hot and sunny they packed up all kinds of delicious food and drink for their picnic some took balls and bats to play beach cricket or volleyball others took small inflatable boats and rubber rings they all took swimming costumes and towels as soon as they arrived at the beach mums and dads could be seen covering their children with sun cream when that operation was complete the children ran onto the beach and down to the water's edge parents followed behind carrying all the things they'd packed into their cars for a fun day out at the seaside.

The boys and girls had decided on a day out at the beach to celebrate the beginning of term**. The** weather forecast was brilliant and the blue skies early on confirmed that it was going to be hot and sunny**. They** packed up all kinds of delicious food and drink for their picnic**. Some** took balls and bats to play beach cricket or volleyball**. Others** took small inflatable boats and rubber rings**. They** all took swimming costumes and towels**. As** soon as they arrived at the beach mums and dads could be seen covering their children with sun cream**. When** that operation was complete the children ran onto the beach and down to the water's edge**. Parents** followed behind carrying all the things they'd packed into their cars for a fun day out at the seaside.

Full stops mark the end of a complete sentence

Look at this sentence:

× The children enjoyed playing on the beach, their parents watched them.

We have two complete sentences here. (If you're not sure what makes a complete sentence look at pages 61–4.) A comma is not strong enough to do the job of separating them.

How can we solve this problem? There are two ways:

- Use a full stop:

✓ The children enjoyed playing on the beach**. Their** parents watched them.

- Use a joining word, such as *and* or *but*:

✓ The children enjoyed playing on the beach **while** their parents watched them.

Quick check

Mask the answers. How would you change the punctuation of these sentences? Unmask the text and check your answers.

1 Sarah helped herself to doughnuts, Lisa thought she was being greedy.

Sarah helped herself to doughnuts**. Lisa** thought she was being greedy.

Sarah helped herself to doughnuts, **but** Lisa thought she was being greedy.

2 Alex applied for the job, he was offered it straight away.

Alex applied for the job**. He** was offered it straight away.

Alex applied for the job **and** was offered it straight away.

3 Sameera spoke three languages at the age of eight, her brother understood two but chose to speak only one.

Sameera spoke three languages at the age of eight**. Her** brother understood two but chose to speak only one.

Sameera spoke three languages at the age of eight, **while** her brother understood two but chose to speak only one.

4 Ed and Emily loved toasted marshmallows, their mum tried to forget this.

Ed and Emily loved toasted marshmallows**. Their** mum tried to forget this.

Ed and Emily loved toasted marshmallows, **but** their mum tried to forget this.

5 The school announced it was closing early, many parents protested.

The school announced it was closing early**. Many** parents protested.

The school announced it was closing early, **and** many parents protested.

6 That film comes out next week, I'd really like to see it.

That film comes out next week**.** I'd really like to see it.

That film comes out next week, **and** I'd really like to see it.

Some special uses of full stops

Use three full stops together to show some words have been missed out or that the sentence just tailed off:

They said they wanted all sorts of things ... I can't remember what exactly.
They felt they had tried everything. They simply didn't know what to do next ...

We used to use full stops after abbreviations:

The B.B.C.
Mr. Jones
H.M.V.
Tennyson Ave.

Some people still use full stops in this way, but you see the following style much more now:

The BBC
Mr Jones
HMV
Tennyson Ave

The general rule here is that every mark we make on the printed page takes up space and makes our writing look more crowded. Readers like a clean airy layout, so it's OK to avoid using full stops after abbreviations as long as this won't create a problem for your readers.

Checklist

- Use full stops to separate complete sentences: *I am hungry. I'd like a sandwich and a glass of water.*
- Use three dots to show that something has been missed out, or that the sentence tails off: *I'm not sure ...*
- Most people now avoid using full stops after abbreviations: *Dr Foster, The WRVS*

Key idea 2: Question marks

Question marks should come at the end of a sentence that is a **direct question** (one that contains the actual words of the question asked).

How much money have you got?
Where is your suitcase?
Did you buy any souvenirs?
Are any of them made from protected species?

Quick check

Mask the answers. Put question marks where needed in these sentences. Unmask the text and check your answers.

1 Do you like butter.

Do you like butter**?**

2 She's my best friend.

She's my best friend. (this is not a direct question)

3 They're late, aren't they.

They're late, aren't they**?**

4 Where's George.

Where's George**?**

5 When does the film start.

When does the film start**?**

Indirect questions

You don't need a question mark after an **indirect question** (one that is reported). Imagine you're helping a friend prepare for an interview. You might say:

I think they'll ask you where you live.

This is an indirect question, so no question mark is needed. If it were asked as a direct question, it would need a question mark:

Where do you live?

You might also say:

I'm sure they'll ask you what you're studying.

Again, this is an indirect question, so no question mark is needed. If it were asked as a direct question, it would need a question mark:

What are you studying?

Take a look at the questions at the top of the previous page. Imagine you were asked them by a customs official when crossing a border on your holiday. Writing to a friend about these questions, you would probably include a series of indirect questions:

They asked me how much money I had.
They wanted to know where my suitcase was.
They checked whether I had bought any souvenirs.
They asked if any of them were made from protected species.

Note that none of these needs a question mark at the end.

Quick check

Mask the answers. Does the sentence need a question mark or a full stop? Unmask the text and check your answers.

1 He asked me if I wanted to go to the cinema

full stop

2 How do you know he won't come

question mark

3 He wants to know where the peas are

full stop

4 How far do they intend to travel

question mark

5 Where do you want to go on holiday next year

question mark

Checklist

- Use a question mark at the end of a sentence that is a direct question: *Do you like red wine? What's the weather like today?*
- Do not use a question mark if the question is indirect: *He asked me if I like red wine. The children wanted to know what the weather is like today.*

Key idea 3: Exclamation marks

Use an exclamation mark at the end of a spoken sentence or phrase that shows strong emotion or urgency.

Help! I'm drowning!
Don't do that again!

We can also use exclamation marks after exclamations of surprise or excitement.

What a fantastic pool!
What a wonderful view from the upstairs windows!

We tend not to use them in formal writing. If you're writing as part of your job, they should rarely be used. They are not out of place in e-mails between close colleagues, but avoid using them when you write to other organizations and people you don't know.

- ✗ Please attend the meeting at 10 o'clock sharp!
- ✗ Never use more than one exclamation mark unless you're writing to a friend!!!!

Quick check

Mask the answers. Put exclamation marks where needed in these sentences. Unmask the text and check your answers.

1 'Don't touch that' said the teacher, pointing at the sulphuric acid.
'Don't touch that**!**' said the teacher, pointing at the sulphuric acid.

2 What a handsome baby boy
What a handsome baby boy**!**

3 'I can't believe you ate that snail' shrieked Emily.
'I can't believe you ate that snail**!**' shrieked Emily.

4 'Did you hear the news? They've won. It's just amazing.'
'Did you hear the news? They've won**!** It's just amazing**!**'

Checklist

- Use exclamation marks when punctuating something someone has said in an excited or urgent way: *Don't even consider it! He's passed his exams! I can't believe it!*
- Avoid exclamation marks in formal writing – a full stop is usually enough: *The managing director announced a significant rise in profits.*

Key idea 4: Commas

Most people understand that a comma marks a break or pause inside a sentence. As a result, people often develop a 'use-a-comma-whenever-you-breathe' policy.

Don't do this. We all breathe at different rates so that can't be a good idea.

So when should you use a comma?

The comma in lists

We use commas to separate items in a list. They make it clear where one item stops and the next starts.

I went to the shops and I bought chocolate, cheese and eggs.
They asked John, Sarah, Alex, Nick and Sophie to the party.

Notice that:

- in these simple lists there is no need for a comma before the word *and*
- there is a space after the comma but no space before the comma

Quick check

Mask the answers. Put commas where needed in these sentences. Unmask the text and check your answers.

1 Please ask Anna Jack and Polly to come to the exhibition.
Please ask Anna**,** Jack and Polly to come to the exhibition.

2 To make the cake we need eggs flour butter sugar and lemons.
To make the cake we need eggs**,** flour**,** butter**,** sugar and lemons.

3 I couldn't find his socks shirts ties shoes or gloves.
I couldn't find his socks**,** shirts**,** ties**,** shoes or gloves.

4 They've left books pens chalk folders and paper for you to use.
They've left books**,** pens**,** chalk**,** folders and paper for you to use.

5 The children have packed story books crayons felt tips and a pencil sharpener.
The children have packed story books**,** crayons**,** felt tips and a pencil sharpener.

More about the comma in lists

Lots of people have been taught – and still remember – the rule 'Don't put a comma before *and*.' This is correct for simple lists, like the ones in the previous exercise, but we shouldn't apply that rule to every list with *and* in it.

Take a look at this sentence:

> They asked for chicken and chips ham and peas tuna and tomatoes and cheese sandwiches.

If we read this list out to someone, we'd group together the words that make up each item. That's the job that commas do in writing. We need to make it clear what is in the sandwiches. Is it just cheese? Is it tomatoes and cheese? Or is it tuna and tomatoes and cheese?

In fact, this is what's on the menu:

> chicken and chips
> ham and peas
> tuna and tomatoes
> cheese sandwiches

So where would you put the commas?

> They asked for chicken and chips, ham and peas, tuna and tomatoes, and cheese sandwiches.

Putting the extra comma between *tomatoes* and *and* makes it clear where one item stops and the next starts.

Quick check

Mask the answers. Put commas where needed in these sentences. Unmask the text and check your answers.

1 I'd like you to put the eggs and cheese in the fridge the tinned dog food in the larder and the bread in the bread bin.

   I'd like you to put the eggs and cheese in the fridge**,** the tinned dog food in the larder**,** and the bread in the bread bin.

2 The man ordered six gin and tonics four whisky and sodas one rum and black and an orange juice each for the children.

   The man ordered six gin and tonics**,** four whisky and sodas**,** one rum and black**,** and an orange juice each for the children.

Using commas to join two sentences

We saw on page 69 that we should not use a comma on its own to separate two sentences. This is correct. But we can use a comma before *but*, *yet*, *and*, *or* and *while* when these words join two sentences.

> Ex-offenders often find it very difficult to get a job, yet it's widely recognised that getting a job helps prevent re-offending.
> Amy and Sarah decided to spend the day shopping, while Mike and Thomas relaxed watching the cricket at the Oval.
> The teachers have said they will not tolerate rude behaviour from pupils, and I won't tolerate it either.

You do not have to use a comma in these sentences. Try reading them aloud with a comma, and then without. You'll hear a different emphasis. In your own writing, you'll have to decide whether to include the comma or not.

Compare these examples with the one on page 69, where I haven't used a comma. It's often two longer sentences that benefit from a comma before the joining word.

Quick check

Mask the answers. Punctuate these sentences to make them easier to read. Unmask the text and check your answers.

1 He ran round and round and his mum couldn't catch him.

He ran round and round**,** and his mum couldn't catch him.

2 The school has a fund to support children from less-well-off families yet the money often stays unclaimed year after year.

The school has a fund to support children from less-well-off families**,** yet the money often stays unclaimed year after year.

3 The British are notoriously bad at learning foreign languages and they miss out on business opportunities because of this.

The British are notoriously bad at learning foreign languages**,** and they miss out on business opportunities because of this.

4 Cathy and Suzanne ordered drinks from the bar while Charles found them a table downstairs.

Cathy and Suzanne ordered drinks from the bar**,** while Charles found them a table downstairs.

Using commas to mark off extra information

Commas are also used to separate the main part of the sentence from extra information, as in these examples:

> John, *the new chief of Police*, created a good impression with the team.
> Anna asked Polly, *her sister*, to keep her a place in the school production.
> The school, *which opened only two months ago*, was burnt to the ground.

In these sentences, the extra information appears between a pair of commas and follows the word it adds to. Notice you could remove that part of the sentence and still have a grammatical sentence left.

If the extra information appears at the end of the sentence then it is sandwiched between a comma and a full stop.

> They chose Nick and Edward, *the two most receptive students*.

If you removed the additional information, the main sentence would still make sense.

> They chose Nick and Edward.

Quick check

Mask the answers. Put commas where necessary into these sentences. (Check you're right by removing the extra information to test whether the sentence still makes sense.) Unmask the text and check your answers.

1 When did Anna the girl with the red top start at the library?
When did Anna**,** the girl with the red top**,** start at the library?

2 The new pool built to the highest specification will open next week.
The new pool**,** built to the highest specification**,** will open next week.

3 The book the best seller this summer was read by the whole family.
The book**,** the best seller this summer**,** was read by the whole family.

4 The managing director Angus Dorg was waiting to see her.
The managing director**,** Angus Dorg**,** was waiting to see her.

5 There's little time left to visit the island one of the last untouched wildernesses.
There's little time left to visit the island**,** one of the last untouched wildernesses.

Commas that mark off information work in pairs

If the extra information is in the middle of the sentence it needs to be sandwiched by a pair of commas. Leaving one of the pair out can cause confusion.

× David, the most promising student in his year worked hard in the library.

The comma after *David* tells us to wait until after a second comma for the verb that goes with the subject. But we reach a full stop before we see a second comma, and so we need to go back and take another look.

There is no such confusion if you remember to add the second of the pair of commas marking off the extra information about David:

✓ David, the most promising student in his year, worked hard in the library.

You might notice a similar problem in this sentence:

× The manager recruited by head office, was not liked by the staff.

The problem here is the single comma after *head office*. It creates a break between the subject and the verb. It is a fixed rule of punctuation that you should **never leave a single comma between a subject and its verb**.

If we add another comma, we fix the problem. The subject – *the new manager* – is now separated from its verb – *was not well received* – by two commas, not one.

✓ The manager, recruited by head office, was not liked by the staff.

Quick check

Mask the answers. Add commas to make these sentences easier to read. Try to spot the main idea of the sentence and use commas to mark off additional information. Unmask the text and check your answers.

1 Alice Smith, the new secretary planned to work hard every day.
Alice Smith, the new secretary**,** planned to work hard every day.

2 He asked Tim his brother's best friend to teach him to play the guitar.
He asked Tim**,** his brother's best friend**,** to teach him to play the guitar.

3 Could the new school smaller than the last one help Jack settle down?
Could the new school**,** smaller than the last one**,** help Jack settle down?

Using commas to mark off less important phrases

A very simple sentence has only one part, expressing the main idea.

I'll build a house for you.

But many sentences fall into two or more parts. In these cases, putting the commas in the right place can help the reader recognize where to pause to understand the sentence easily.

If I win the lottery, I'll build a house for you.

The comma here marks the end of one part of the sentence and the beginning of another. Sentences with *if* in them often need a comma to show the reader the best place to pause.

If education is to improve teachers need to be paid more.

Without knowing where to pause, it's easy to read this sentence wrongly. We might start off thinking the writer is talking about what needs to happen *If education is to improve teachers* ... But the words that follow – *need to be paid more* – tell us we need to re-read and re-phrase the sentence to make sense of it.

A well-placed comma makes the sentence clearer.

If education is to improve, teachers need to be paid more.

Here are some other examples of how a comma separates the main idea from a less important part of the sentence, and helps the reader to group the words correctly and understand them straight away. The words in italic type are the main part of the sentence:

Because he was so ill, *he had to stay in hospital for a week.*
Now that you are here, *we need to ask you some questions.*

Quick check

Mask the answers. Add commas to make these sentences easier to read. Unmask the text and check your answers.

1 If the store agrees to take him on he's bound to do well.

If the store agrees to take him on**,** he's bound to do well.

2 If the Wilsons arrive on the 4pm flight they'll have to stay the night in London before going to Cornwall.

If the Wilsons arrive on the 4pm flight**,** they'll have to stay the night in London before going to Cornwall.

Now really test yourself

Add commas to make these sentences easier to read. Check your answers on page 211.

1 They wanted to have a range of sandwiches available: cheese and pickle beef and gherkin tuna and mayonnaise and brie and grapes.

2 Alice prepared all the equipment they needed for the trip and Felix and Nigel got the food ready.

3 If you can explain to me how you happen to have a crocodile skin handbag in your suitcase I will consider what action we take next.

4 Because train journeys in France are so smooth and reasonably priced it's worth considering abandoning your car for the summer.

5 Following the recent downpours and flooding the council has decided to invest more money in flood protection barriers.

6 He had brought sandwiches pies scotch eggs dips ice creams cakes sweets and fruit.

Checklist

- In simple lists use commas to separate the items. In simple lists you do not need a comma before the word *and* that links the last item: *He asked Father Christmas for crayons, a train set and a story book.*
- In more complex lists with longer items, use a comma to separate all the items, including the last item linked by *and*: *She asked Father Christmas for a doll with a full wardrobe, a red sports car for the doll, a make-up bag, a new princess dress trimmed with sequins, and a DVD.*
- You can use a comma before *and*, *but*, *while*, *yet* and *or* when these words link two sentences. But you don't have to – read the sentence aloud to decide which is best: *Vegans eat only food that can be grown in soil, but vegetarians eat dairy products and fish as well.*
- Use a pair of commas to separate the main part of the sentence from extra information: *Their new teacher, a tall young man, had a great sense of humour.*
- Use a comma to separate the main part of a sentence from a less important part, to help the reader see how the words need to be grouped to make sense: *Before they left the office after the Christmas party, they cleared away all the empty bottles and tidied up all the leftovers.*

Key idea 5: Colons

A colon consists of two dots one on top of the other (:). Don't leave a space before it, but always leave a space after. The word that comes next after a colon usually starts with a small letter rather than a capital.

A colon might be used to mark a pause before a list. In this sentence the words after the colon detail what was bought:

> He went to the shops and bought everything they'd need for dinner: eggs, bacon, tomatoes, potatoes, salad, bread and fruit.

A colon might also be used before an explanation. In this sentence the phrase after the colon explains what the good advice was:

> He gave me some good advice: never a lender or a borrower be.

Here are some other examples of how a colon can be used before an explanation:

> They were taught the essentials of safe cycling on the roads: look, signal, look again and then move off.
> They chose a better route: one that avoided all the overcrowded motorways.

Quick check

Mask the answers. Put colons where needed in these sentences. Unmask the text and check your answers.

1 There are many reasons you can't go on the school trip it's not very educational, it costs too much money, none of your friends are going and you don't get on with the teacher who's leading the group.

There are many reasons you can't go on the school trip**:** it's not very educational, it costs too much money, none of your friends are going and you don't get on with the teacher who's leading the group.

2 He explained the key areas to think about before travelling abroad getting inoculations in good time, planning how to get money throughout the trip and learning at least a few phrases in the language of each country you intend to visit.

He explained the key areas to think about before travelling abroad**:** getting inoculations in good time, planning how to get money throughout the trip and learning at least a few phrases in the language of each country you intend to visit.

Now really test yourself

Add colons to make these sentences easier to read. Check your answers on pages 211–2.

1 He asked the first students in the register to help Andrew, Jane, Guy, Tim and Cathy.

2 They couldn't believe all the things they needed to buy for the first-aid kit bandages, plasters, antiseptic spray, antiseptic cream, triangular bandages, pain-killing tablets ... to name but a few items.

3 The leaflet told us what to do in an emergency power cut make our way to the exit calmly and hold the hand of the person in front of and behind us.

4 They showed us how much they enjoyed the dinner we had prepared they ate every morsel.

5 She loved every aspect of the garden sitting in it, weeding it, picking salad leaves and simply admiring it.

6 They presented us with quite a choice of holiday destinations Cuba, The Seychelles, Egypt or Venezuela.

7 He worked incredibly hard throughout his stay he did the garden, renewed the fencing and painted the window frames.

8 The invitation promised a fantastic evening delicious food, plenty of fine wine, a midnight swim and a jazz band.

9 She made it clear she didn't intend to stay she packed her suitcase and ordered a taxi for the airport.

10 Go and gather together everything you need for the trip wet gear, shorts, swimming things, sun tan cream, walking shoes, trainers and sandals.

Checklist

- Colons tell the reader that an explanation or more detail is coming: *A well-fitting cycle helmet can save lives: statistics show that if you're wearing a helmet when you fall off your bike, you're more likely to survive.*
- Colons are often used before a list: *He invited his very best friends to meet his family: James, John, Anna and Jack.*

Key idea 6: Apostrophes

The apostrophe can arouse strong reactions in people. It can cause passion, irritation and apathy. Even if we don't feel strongly about them ourselves, it's useful to know how to use them correctly in case we run into people who do.

There are two places where we need apostrophes:

- to show a letter or letters have been missed out
- to show possession – that something belongs to someone or something

Apostrophes show missing letters

When words are shortened an apostrophe is put in the place where letters have been left out.

I'm (= I am – the apostrophe replaces the letter *a*)
he's (= he is – the apostrophe replaces the letter *i*)
he's (= he has – the apostrophe replaces the letters *ha*)
you're (= you are – the apostrophe replaces the letter *a*)
we're (= we are – the apostrophe replaces the letter *a*)
they'll (= they will – the apostrophe replaces the letters *wi*)
it's (= it is – the apostrophe replaces the letter *i*)
it's (= it has – the apostrophe replaces the letters *ha*)

> **Remember:** The apostrophe in *it's* shows missing letters. This is one of the most troublesome problems in English.

Putting apostrophes into our writing to show missing letters allows our writing to reflect how we speak. This is fine if you want to be friendly and informal. But in formal writing we don't usually use apostrophes to show missing letters: instead we write the complete words.

If I wanted to be friendly and informal I might write:

We'd like to invite you to an interview.
You'll need to bring your CV with you.

But to be formal I would write:

We would like to invite you to an interview.
You will need to bring your CV with you.

Quick check

Mask the answers. Put in apostrophes where necessary to indicate missing letters. Unmask the text and check your answers.

1 Its too late to ask him to bring plates.
It's (it is) too late to ask him to bring plates.

2 Why havent they offered more time?
Why haven't (have not) they offered more time?

3 Were in the garden every evening.
We're (we are) in the garden every evening.

4 Youre away from next week until the end of January.
You're (you are) away from next week until the end of January.

5 She wanted to know why theyre so important.
She wanted to know why they're (they are) so important.

6 Hes ten years old next October.
He's (he is) ten years old next October.

7 Wheres the form gone?
Where's (where has) the form gone?

8 Whys he waiting? The lights have changed.
Why's (why is) he waiting? The lights have changed.

9 Whos he going to the dance with?
Who's (who is) he going to the dance with?

10 Whens the next train?
When's (when is) the next train?

Apostrophes show possession

Apostrophes also show that one thing belongs to or is associated with another.

the boy's bag (= the bag belonging to the boy)
the book's cover (= the cover of the book)

The book does not actually 'own' its cover – but the term 'possession' is useful as it helps us see the relationship between the two nouns.

Placing the apostrophe

One of the problems people have with apostrophes is working out where they need to go. In fact it's not that hard if you follow two simple steps.

The first step is to work out who or what is in possession. We can call these the 'possessors'. I have put the possessors in bold type in the examples below:

the boy's bag (= the bag belonging to **the boy**)
the book's cover (= the cover of **the book**)

The second step is to add the apostrophe. The apostrophe always goes right after the possessor – not necessarily at the end of the word:

the boy's bag
the book's cover

Quick check

Mask the answers. Work out the possessor in each of these and insert an apostrophe in the correct place. Unmask the text and check your answers.

1 the towns churches

the town's churches

2 Alans job

Alan's job

3 Sarahs room

Sarah's room

4 the Presidents strategy

the President's strategy

5 I'll give you one days notice.

I'll give you **one day**'s notice.

More on placing the apostrophe

Now look at these examples:

the teachers' timetable	(= the timetable belonging to **the teachers**)
the three ministers' cars	(= the cars belonging to **the three ministers**)

I have again put the possessors in bold. The only difference is that the possessors here are all plural and end in *-s*.

And – exactly as before – if I use an apostrophe to show possession, the apostrophe goes immediately after the possessor:

the teachers' timetable
the three ministers' cars

You can work through the same two steps whenever you use an apostrophe to show possession. Where should the apostrophe go in this phrase?

the mens race

Work through the stages. First work out who or what is the possessor – in this case *the men* – and then put the apostrophe immediately after it.

the men's race

Quick check

Mask the answers. Work out the possessor in each case and insert an apostrophe in the correct place. Unmask the text and check your answers.

1 in all the employees opinion

in **all the employees**' opinion

2 the twin sisters room

the twin sisters' room

3 these gardens best features

these gardens' best features

4 the childrens breakfast

the children's breakfast

5 the womens decision

the women's decision

Some traps involving apostrophes

Beware of the temptation to put apostrophes where they don't belong. One place where this might happen is with words like *theirs*, *yours*, *his*, *hers* and *ours*.

Do these words ever need an apostrophe? The answer is 'no'. The reason for this is they already mean 'belonging to'. (Remember that when we looked at them on page 55 we called them *possessive* pronouns.) Because the idea of possession is included in these words, there is no need to add an apostrophe.

Whose book is this?
It's theirs
No. It's ours.

People are sometimes tempted to put apostrophes in any word that ends in *-s*. What about this sentence?

The apples are in the bowl.

Does it need any apostrophes? Ask yourself:

- are there any missing letters?
- are any of the words ending in *-s* possessors?

The answer to both questions is 'no', so no apostrophes are needed in this sentence. Not every word that ends in *-s* needs to have an apostrophe.

Quick check

Mask the answers. Are these sentences correct? Improve any incorrect sentences by putting in or taking out apostrophes. Unmask the text and check your answers.

1 The ministers took their decision quickly.
correct

2 The ministers late for the meeting.
incorrect (the minister's)

3 The ministers decision was praised by her colleagues.
incorrect (the minister's)

4 Its a shame.
incorrect (it's)

5 You all need to have your visas stamped before you leave the country.
correct

Now really test yourself

Correct any sentences that are wrong by putting in apostrophes where needed. Check your answers on page 212.

1 The days events were recorded on camera.

2 The headteachers solution was to take on more staff.

3 The cats not well so I must take her to see the vet.

4 This companys key assets were its staff and expertise.

5 These companies key assets are their premises and stock.

6 The companies have joined forces.

7 The managers agreed to implement the new strategy.

8 Whos going to tell her why youre late?

9 The doctors dont want to increase their patients waiting time.

10 Cant you see hes not doing the invoices accurately?

11 The weathers been great throughout the holiday.

12 The team members enthusiasm helped them do their best.

13 The dog chased its tail for half an hour.

14 The children ran right up to the waters edge.

15 Its got to have its claws clipped.

Checklist

- Apostrophes show either missing letters or possession.
- When the apostrophe shows possession, work out who the 'possessor' is and place the apostrophe immediately after it.
- Not every word that ends in *-s* needs to have an apostrophe.

Some final thoughts about good punctuation

Remember that punctuation is there to help the reader. This part of the book should have given you a clear idea of the reasons for using the main punctuation marks:

- full stops
- question marks
- exclamation marks
- commas
- colons
- apostrophes

Check back if you need to remind yourself about any of these.

Finally, keep in mind these tips for good punctuation:

- Never put a space before a full stop, a question mark, an exclamation mark, a comma or a colon.
- Always leave a single space after a full stop, a question mark, an exclamation mark, a comma or a colon.
- The full stop should be your most frequently used mark of punctuation.
- The golden rule: use punctuation sparingly: if in doubt, leave it out.

Now really test yourself

Add punctuation to this passage so that a reader can make sense of it easily. Check your answer on page 213.

The Mayor asked the people at the meeting what they thought of wind farms hands shot up and people offered a range of opinions some said they were ugly others that they made too much noise and a few that they could help slow the rise in sea level when everyone had said their bit the Mayor spoke again and confirmed the council had agreed to site a wind farm on Golden Hill there were shouts cries and some applause from the audience but silence reigned when he shouted out that the rent from the land would allow the council to build a modern hospital with all the latest equipment for the town.

PART C

EASILY CONFUSED WORDS

Similar sounding words aren't always written the same

There are many words in English that sound exactly the same as or similar to another word. When we're speaking to someone, this tends not to cause a problem. We can usually tell if the person we're talking to hasn't understood because they frown or look puzzled or may even ask us to repeat or explain what we've said.

But it is not so easy to get away with confusing two words when we are writing words down. If we spell them wrongly we can cause confusion – and we may not be on the spot to sort this confusion out.

For example, if we are confused about the difference between the words *for* and *four*, it won't make any difference when we speak. But if we write *for* when we mean *four* it might make a lot of difference. If we are lucky, whoever is reading it may wonder what on earth we mean; if we are unlucky, they may think we mean something other than what we intended to write.

What can you get out of this section?

It will:

- show you words and phrases that are often confused
- explain the difference between them
- let you practise until you're happy you can use the right word

Just do the exercises you need to!

I've gathered together a range of words that often get confused. If you already know the difference between the words, the exercises will probably seem ridiculously easy, so – like the rest of this part of the book – just practise the ones you know you might slip up on.

accept / except / expect

These are three different words. Make sure you don't write one when you mean one of the others.

The word ***accept*** is a verb that means 'to take something that is offered to you'.

> He *accepted* her kind offer of a lift home.
> I won't *accept* such a poor standard of work from you.

The word ***except*** means 'not including'.

> Everyone *except* John got top marks.
> He'll eat anything *except* liver.

The word ***expect*** is a verb that means 'to think something is going to happen'.

> I *expect* him to arrive around 7 tonight.
> England *expects* every man to do his duty.

Tip: It may help you to remember that ***except*** is part of ***excep****tion* and ***accept*** is part of ***accep****tance*.

Now test yourself

Put *accept*, *except* or *expect* in the gap to complete each sentence. You can check your answers on page 214.

1 Do you ______ me to help you mow the lawn?

2 Most students ______ their results without complaint.

3 He was delighted to ______ the award for his research.

4 They saw everything in Paris ______ the Eiffel Tower.

5 Do you ______ that you need to work harder?

6 Please don't ______ him to bring anything.

7 What do you ______ if you don't study all year?

8 They chose to ______ the offer of compensation.

advice / advise

These are two different parts of the same word: one is the noun, the other is the verb. Make sure you don't write one when you mean the other.

The word ***advice*** is a noun. We give ***advice*** to people to help them do something better.

My *advice* to you is to phone the police immediately.
The man followed his doctor's *advice* to the letter.

The word ***advise*** is a verb. When we ***advise*** someone, we tell them what we think they ought to do.

The estate agent *advised* the couple to redecorate the kitchen.
I would *advise* you to hand in your homework on time.

Tip: It may help you to remember you use **s** to write the verb, and **c** to write the noun. You can hear the difference.

Now test yourself

Put either *advice* or *advise* in the gap to complete each sentence. You can check your answers on page 214.

1 I would ______ you to go to the doctor.

2 They won't listen to my ______.

3 Please follow the man's ______. He knows what he's talking about.

4 I had to ______ him not to buy the car.

5 Do you have any ______ about what to wear to this interview?

6 My ______ to you is to do what you are told.

7 If they continue to ignore her ______, she'll stop helping them.

8 We ______ all UK citizens to contact the British Embassy.

9 I would ______ all my students to read regularly.

10 We always ______ travellers to check what vaccinations they need.

affect / effect

These are two different words. Make sure you don't write one when you mean the other.

The word ***affect*** is a verb that means 'to change or to alter'.

The documentary about the war *affected* his whole life.
The bad weather this summer won't *affect* how I feel about France.

The word ***effect*** is a noun meaning 'result'.

The *effect* of heating water is to create steam.
The *effects* of the accident at Chernobyl are still being felt.

> **Tip:** It may help you to remember that ***a****ffect* and ***a****lter* both begin with ***a***.

Now test yourself

Put either *affect* or *effect* in the gap to complete each sentence. You can check your answers on page 215.

1 His speech had a great ______ on the children in the audience.

2 The ______ of water on iron is rust.

3 The Holocaust Exhibition will surely ______ all who visit it.

4 What ______ do you get if you splash the walls with red and blue paint?

5 The new documents failed to ______ the minister's opinion.

6 How does the heat usually ______ you?

7 The ______ of prolonged exposure to sunshine is sunburn.

8 For many the ______ of consuming too much butter is increased levels of cholesterol in the blood.

9 Mosquito bites don't ______ some people, but others can't stop scratching.

10 Scientists can't agree what ______ mobile phones have on the brain.

alternative / alternate

These are two different words. Make sure you don't write one when you mean the other.

The word ***alternative*** is a noun and adjective indicating another way of doing something.

What are the *alternatives* to going by car?
We have no *alternative* strategy.

The word ***alternate*** is a verb and adjective used when you mean 'first one, then the other'.

We play tennis on *alternate* weeks.
They usually *alternate* between playing rounders and baseball.

Now test yourself

Put either *alternative* or *alternate* in the gap to complete each sentence. You can check your answers on page 215.

1 They are trying to find an ______ to nuclear power.

2 It's not fair if one person does it every week. They should ______.

3 Have you explored every ______ ?

4 His shirt has ______ stripes of pink and pale blue.

5 Sarah favours ______ medicine rather than conventional medicines.

6 There should be an ______ to chips on the menu.

7 The weather tended to ______ between snow and sunshine.

8 They hold gym classes on ______ Saturdays.

9 Is there any ______ to prison?

10 The boys ______ between being rude to us and ignoring us.

are / our

These are two different words. Make sure you don't write one when you mean the other.

The word ***are*** is used with *there*, *we*, *they*, *you* and plural nouns. It is part of the verb *be*.

They *are* late.
There *are* five plates on the table.
Those children *are* lucky!

The word ***our*** means 'belonging to us'. It is part of the same family of words as *my*, *your*, *his*, *her*, *its* and *their* – all words that say who or what something belongs to.

Our house is in the middle of our street.
Our method is the best.
They like *our* garden.

> **Tip:** It may help you to remember that ***ou***r means 'belonging t***o u***s'.

Now test yourself

Put either *our* or *are* in the gap to complete each sentence. You can check your answers on page 216.

1 They came to ______ house.

2 The vet said we could not take ______ cat home.

3 ______ you ready yet?

4 ______ potatoes are the best on the allotment.

5 ______ the courses starting next week?

6 ______ new courses ______ very popular.

7 There ______ two parks in the city centre.

8 They ______ delighted with the flowers.

9 Where is ______ dinner?

10 Where ______ ______ friends?

borrow / lend

These words mean two different things. Make sure you don't write one when you mean the other.

The word ***borrow*** means 'to take something from someone with their permission'. Remember you borrow something *from* someone.

He *borrowed* all the books he could find.
My father won't *borrow* anything from anyone.

The word ***lend*** means to give something to someone for a short time. Remember you lend something *to* someone.

I'm happy to *lend* this to you, but just for a week.
The local library *lends* books free of charge.

> **Tip:** It may help you to remember that when a bank ***lends*** money, this is called a ***l***oan.

Now test yourself

Put either *borrow* or *lend* in the gap to complete each sentence. You can check your answers on page 216.

1 She wants to ______ my hairdryer.

2 Jane wouldn't ______ her new fountain pen to her friend.

3 If I ______ you this book, can you ______ me your new CD?

4 He asked to ______ my casserole dish and never gave it back.

5 Alex was able to ______ everything he needed to go camping.

6 Why don't you ______ him your new torch?

7 Please ______ me your MP3 player for the journey.

8 He needs to ______ money from the bank to open a shop.

9 The bank will ______ him the money because they know he'll succeed.

10 My grandma used to say, '______ to save and you'll always have plenty.'

bought / brought

These are two different words. They sound similar. Make sure you don't write one when you mean the other.

Bought is a form of the verb *buy* which means 'to get something in exchange for money'.

> I *bought* some hand cream at the chemist's.
> He *bought* a large pot plant at the florist's.

Brought is a form of the verb *bring* which means 'to carry something to a place'.

> They *brought* their children with them.
> What have you *brought* with you to eat?

> **Tip:** It may help you to remember that *bought* is from *buy*, so it has no ***r***, but *b**r**ought* is from *b**r**ing*, so it does have an ***r***.

Now test yourself

Put either *bought* or *brought* in the gap to complete each sentence. You can check your answers on page 217.

1 What did you buy at the market? I ______ nothing.

2 For the camping weekend he______lots of things from his larder.

3 How many new computers has the school ______?

4 They have ______ lots of new clothes in the sales.

5 The children ______ their favourite toys to play with.

6 European explorers ______ new diseases to South America.

7 They've spent two hours at the shops. What have they ______?

8 Have they ______ their tent with them?

9 I've ______ some visitors to cheer you up.

10 I can't believe he's ______ another one from eBay!

break / brake

These are two different words, but they sound the same. Make sure you don't write one when you mean the other.

The word ***break*** is a verb that means 'to make something not work' or 'to smash into pieces'. It can also be a noun that means 'a change of activity or a short holiday'. *Broke* and *broken* are forms of the verb *break* that you use when talking about past time.

He said he didn't *break* the cup. I don't believe him.
They went to Prague for a weekend *break*.
I *broke* the cup.
She *has broken* her leg.

The word ***brake*** is the name of the control in a vehicle that makes it stop. It can be used as a verb meaning 'to slow down'. *Braked* is a form of the verb *brake* that you use when talking about past time.

These *brakes* don't work properly.
He turned the corner and had to *brake* suddenly to avoid crashing.
She *braked* sharply at the traffic lights.

Tip: It may help you to remember that *rakes* don't have *brakes*.

Now test yourself

Put either *break* or *brake* (or a form of one of these) in the gap to complete each sentence. You can check your answers on page 217.

1 On a bike it's best to ______ gently.

2 The doctor has recommended he take a ______ from work.

3 The bus driver had to ______ to avoid hitting the dog.

4 Taking a weekend ______ abroad has got much cheaper.

5 How did you ______ the lid of that casserole dish?

6 Last year when he went skiing he ______ his arm.

7 I've been working on this for hours and I need a ______.

8 He ______ suddenly when he saw the police car ahead.

breathe / breath / breadth

These are three different words. Make sure you don't write one when you mean one of the others.

The word ***breathe*** is a verb that means 'to take air into your lungs'.

He could scarcely *breathe* after finishing his first marathon.
The hot weather makes it difficult to *breathe*.

The word ***breath*** is a noun meaning 'the air you take in and out of your lungs'.

His *breath* smelt sweet.
It was so cold he could see his *breath* as it left his mouth.

The word ***breadth*** is a noun meaning 'the size of something measured from side to side'.

Measure the *breadth* and then multiply this by the length.
The result was greeted with cheers the length and *breadth* of country.

> **Tip:** It may help you to remember that you should breath**e** **e**asily.

Now test yourself

Put *breath*, *breathe* or *breadth* in the gap to complete each sentence. You can check your answers on pages 217–8.

1 He ran out of ______ after the first lap.

2 When they found the missing keys I heard them ______ a sigh of relief.

3 The doctor told him to take a deep ______.

4 You can help stop yourself falling asleep if you take a deep ______.

5 The children measured the ______ and the height of their tent.

6 It can be difficult to ______ when you're wearing a mask.

7 They could scarcely ______ because the smoke was so thick.

8 How long can you hold your ______ under water?

hear / here

These are two different words. Make sure you don't write one when you mean the other.

The word ***hear*** is a verb that explains what our ears do.

Can you *hear* the noise?
They *hear* mice chewing the floorboards at night.
Jane can't *hear* you. She's wearing headphones.
I didn't *hear* him say that.

The word ***here*** means 'in this place' or 'to this place'.

Do you live *here*?
He came *here* at 12 o'clock.
Where are the books on local history? *Here* on this shelf.
I was born *here*.

Tip: It may help you to remember that we h***ear*** with our ***ear***s.

Now test yourself

Put either *hear* or *here* in the gap to complete each sentence. You can check your answers on page 218.

1 Where's the ball? It's over ______.

2 Can you ______ me at the back?

3 I didn't ______ what you said.

4 They'll ______ you if you speak clearly.

5 ______ comes John.

6 The letters to the school are ______.

7 They don't like living ______.

8 If you keep talking I won't ______ what they're saying on the radio.

9 ______ are the last letters for you to sign.

10 We need to stick to the ______ and now.

it's / its

These are two different words. Make sure you don't write one when you mean the other. Maybe I should also mention here that the word ***its'*** does not exist. **Anywhere!**

The word ***its*** means 'belonging to it'. It is part of the same family of words as *my*, *your*, *his*, *her*, *our* and *their* – all words that say who or what something belongs to.

The table was modern. *Its* legs were made of steel.
The cat wasn't well. *Its* fur looked dull and moth-eaten.
The course claimed that *its* aim was to help children cycle safely.

The word ***it's*** is short for 'it is' or 'it has'.

It's lovely weather today.
It's been ages since we last saw you.
It's a great shame they did that.

Tip: Remember that the apostrophe is used to show a missing letter or letters.

Now test yourself

Put either *its* or *it's* in the gap to complete each sentence. You can check your answers on pages 218–9.

1 ______ been a lovely holiday.

2 The house is too small and ______ garden is too big.

3 ______ not something I would ever consider.

4 The monster approached. ______ head was green and slimy.

5 ______ never too late to learn something new.

6 ______ a disaster.

7 This book is great. ______ all about the Pacific Ocean.

8 James says ______ best to arrive before 10 o'clock.

9 The house was horrid. ______ walls were painted yucky green.

10 ______ never going to be ready on time.

licence / license

These are two different parts of the same word: one is the noun, the other is the verb. Make sure you don't write one when you mean the other.

The word ***licence*** is a noun. You need a ***licence*** to drive a car and for your television.

My driving *licence* expires in 2006. How do I renew it?
Our television *licence* is renewed automatically each year.

The word ***license*** is a verb. To be ***licensed*** means 'to have permission to do something'.

The bar was *licensed* to sell alcohol.
The premises were *licensed* to stay open until 2am.

Tip: It may help you to remember you use **s** to write the verb, and **c** to write the noun. You can hear the difference between the noun *advi**c**e* and the verb *advi**s**e*.

Now test yourself

Put either *licence* or *licensed* in the gap to complete each sentence. You can check your answers on page 219.

1 They've applied for a ______ to stay open late.

2 This ______ allows you to serve alcohol daily between 7 and 11pm.

3 They granted him a ______ to fish on the River Test.

4 The premises were first ______ 40 years ago.

5 Do you have to be ______ to sell certain chemicals?

6 Apply for your new driving ______ now.

7 If you don't have a TV ______, you're bound to be caught.

8 Have you got a ______ to drive that lorry?

9 The police decided not to renew the bar's ______.

10 The bar had applied to be ______ to serve alcohol 24 hours a day.

lie / lay

These are two different words. Make sure you don't write one when you mean the other.

The word ***lie*** is a verb that means 'to be in a flat position'. The different forms of the verb are *lies*, *lying*, *lay* and *lain*.

Are you going to *lie* in bed all day?
He got to the beach and *lay* down on a towel.
He hasn't *lain* in bed all day for years.

The word ***lay*** is also a verb, and it means 'to put down carefully'. Unlike *lie*, it must have an object to make the sense complete (see page 61). The different forms of the verb are *lays*, *laying* and *laid*.

I'd like you to *lay* the table.
The chicken *laid* an egg.
The boy *laid* his sleeping brother gently on the quilt.

Notice that if you are talking about past time, *lay* is a form of *lie*, but if you are talking about the present time it has a different meaning.

Now test yourself

Put either *lie* or *lay* (or one of the forms of either verb) in the gap to complete each sentence. You can check your answers on pages 219–20.

1 Why don't you ______ and relax on the sofa for half an hour?

2 He ______ the map out on the car bonnet and studied the route.

3 The geese have ______ their eggs early this year.

4 Even the best ______ plans don't always work!

5 They picked up the baby and then ______ him gently down in his cot.

6 How long have you ______ there?

7 How long did you ______ there before the ambulance came?

8 He forgot to ______ a place at the table for Fred.

9 Please let me ______ here a little longer.

10 They opened up the kit and ______ the instruction sheet on the ground.

lit / lighted

These are both the part of the same word, but they are usually used slightly differently in British English.

The word ***lit*** is the form of the verb *light* that is used when talking about past events.

He *lit* the candles before the guests arrived.
They piled loads of branches and dead leaves onto the bonfire and then *lit* it.

The word ***lighted*** is used as an adjective meaning 'having been set light to'. Remember that, as an adjective, this form of the word is always used to describe a noun.

The *lighted* fires flickered in the dark.
The people all carried *lighted* candles.

Now test yourself

Put either *lit* or *lighted* in the gap to complete each sentence. You can check your answers on page 220.

1 He struck a match and ______ the night lights.

2 They ______ the barbeque in plenty of time to cook the food.

3 How many ______ candles were there on his cake?

4 How is the hall ______?

5 They ______ the bonfire all around its base.

6 It is dangerous to play with ______ matches.

7 The moon ______ the surface of the water.

8 Never return to a firework after you have ______ it.

9 She ______ another cigarette.

10 Keith was standing in the ______ window.

lose / loose

These are two different words. Make sure you don't write one when you mean the other.

The word ***lose*** is a verb that means 'to forget where you put something'.

If you *lose* your wallet you should cancel your credit cards immediately.
Don't *lose* your passport when you're on holiday.

The word ***loose*** is an adjective meaning 'not close-fitting' or 'separate'. It's the opposite of *tight*.

His trousers were so *loose* that I was afraid they might fall down.
They have a very *loose* arrangement. Nothing's written down on paper.

Now test yourself

Put either *lose* or *loose* in the gap to complete each sentence. You can check your answers on pages 220–1.

1 Can't you tell if a size 20 is going to be too ______ for you?

2 The doctor has said they need to go on a diet and ______ a few kilos.

3 If you ______ your birth certificate it takes ages to replace it.

4 He was driving along and the engine started to ______ power.

5 I prefer ______ leaf tea to tea bags.

6 Her muscles are very ______ from all the yoga she does.

7 He was determined not to ______ the car keys.

8 I'm not going to ______ any sleep over it.

9 She always has some ______ change in her purse.

10 If they keep shouting, George will ______ it completely.

no / know / now

These are three different words. Make sure you don't write one when you mean one of the others. The words ***no*** and ***know*** sound the same.

The word ***no*** means 'the opposite of *yes*'.

Can I have an ice cream? No.
Do you want to do your homework now? No.

The word ***know*** is a verb that explains **knowledge** someone has in their head.

She doesn't *know* how to boil an egg.
Do you *know* if this is right?

The word ***now*** means 'at this moment' or 'immediately'.

Why put off until tomorrow something you can do *now*?
Now and again we find letters the sender hasn't signed.

> **Tip:** It may help you to remember the noun ***know****ledge* contains the verb ***know***.

Now test yourself

Put *now*, *know* or *no* in the gap to complete each sentence. You can check your answers on page 221.

1 Do you ______ what time it is?

2 I'm sorry, but I can't do it ______.

3 Did they say you could start now? ______, they didn't.

4 You should already ______ the difference between right and wrong.

5 Do you ______ the answer? ______, I don't.

6 When do you finish work? ______. I'm getting ready to leave.

7 How did he ______ you were late?

8 There is ______ butter left.

of / off / have

These are three different words. Make sure you don't write one when you mean one of the others. The words *of* and *have* can sometimes sound the same in spoken English, but they do not mean the same.

The word ***of*** is often used when you are talking about a part of a larger unit.

a bottle *of* gin
a bucket *of* water

The word ***off*** means 'the opposite of *on*'.

He fell *off* the wall!
I can't get this label *off* the box.

The word ***have*** is a verb and can be used with *must*, *can* or *should* when we are expressing how certain we are of something. Note that you should never write *can't of*, *must of* or *should of*.

I can't *have* dreamt it.
He must *have* paid the money into his account last week.

> **Tip:** If you need *have* to form the question, then you should write *have* in the answer: '***Have*** *they finished?' 'No. They can't* ***have***.'

Now test yourself

Put *have*, *off* or *of* in the gap to complete each sentence. You can check your answers on page 221.

1 He took the top ______ the bottle with his new corkscrew.

2 He put a ribbon around the top ______ the bottle.

3 The recipe needs a kilo ______ flour.

4 They must ______ sold the cottage.

5 He could ______ told me you didn't want to go.

6 Get______the table or you'll fall.

7 Sarah might ______ told them the secret.

8 They couldn't ______ got there first.

practice / practise

These are two different parts of the same word: one is the noun, the other is the verb. Make sure you don't write one when you mean the other.

The word ***practice*** is a noun meaning 'doing something a number of times to improve' or 'the process of doing something'.

I went to tennis *practice* last night.
The *practice* of pressing grapes with your feet has almost died out.

The word ***practise*** is a verb meaning 'to do something a number of times to improve'.

She *practised* her lines until she was word perfect.
They liked *practising* their set pieces on the football pitch after work.

Tip: It may help you to remember you use **s** to write the verb, and **c** to write the noun. You can hear the difference between the noun *advi***c***e* and the verb *advi***s***e*.

Now test yourself

Put either *practice* or *practise* in the gap to complete each sentence. You can check your answers on page 222.

1 He needs to ______ regularly to improve his guitar playing.

2 The ______ of bear-baiting was outlawed only a century ago.

3 There is a football ______ after school.

4 They had to ______ for the concert for weeks.

5 This tennis ______ has not helped him get rid of his problems serving.

6 I haven't decided whether to go to the ______ this week.

7 John needs to ______ making scones.

8 My grandma always said, '______ makes perfect!'

9 My father always says, '______ what you preach!'

10 If you ______ , your playing will improve.

quiet / quite

These are two different words. Make sure you don't write one when you mean the other.

The word ***quiet*** means 'without much noise'.

It's *quiet* here in the evenings.
You must be very *quiet* when people are working.
Sophie is a *quiet* child.

The word ***quite*** means 'fairly', or 'very', or it can show the speaker agrees.

He's *quite* incredible for his age.
Do you want to go? I'd *quite* like to.
'So it's all over, then?' '*Quite*.'

Now test yourself

Put either *quite* or *quiet* in the gap to complete each sentence. You can check your answers on page 222.

1 He's ______ unhappy when he goes into kennels.

2 Be ______. You're making too much noise.

3 The children are playing in the park, so the house is ______.

4 He's ______ friendly and always waves when he sees me.

5 Teachers like the class to be ______ while they take the register.

6 He was ______ calm immediately after the accident.

7 He said the film was ______ good so I'd like to see it.

8 I think that's ______ unfair.

9 I'm sure you can be really ______ if you try!

10 The engine's so ______ I can't hear when I've stalled.

stationary / stationery

These are two different words. Make sure you don't write one when you mean the other.

The word ***stationary*** is an adjective that means 'not moving'.

> The car was *stationary*.
> When the clock chimed every vehicle was *stationary*.
> *Stationary* vehicles may cause a considerable nuisance.

The word ***stationery*** is a noun meaning 'all the things you need to write'.

> His *stationery* order included five sizes of envelope!
> Most organizations could save money if they controlled *stationery* carefully.
> They spent a fortune on elaborate *stationery*.

> **Tip:** It may help you to remember that station**e**ry includes **e**nvelopes, and that c**a**rs are sometimes station**a**ry.

Now test yourself

Put either *stationary* or *stationery* in the gap to complete each sentence. You can check your answers on page 223.

1 I thought the car was_______so I turned right in front of it.

2 Please check who is responsible for ______.

3 The_______cupboard key has gone missing.

4 When cycling watch out for the doors of ______ vehicles!

5 They've had the bill for last month's ______.

6 The customs officials asked them to remain ______.

7 I couldn't tell from that distance whether the car was ______ or not.

8 Make a list of all the ______ you need for your department.

9 Never cross the road between two ______ vehicles.

10 Put the ______ order in by the 10th of every month.

there / their / they're

These are three different words. They all sound the same. Make sure you don't write one when you mean one of the others.

The word ***there*** often goes with *is*, *are*, *was* and *were*. It also means 'in that place'.

There are six chairs around the table.
There were 500 people at the meeting last night.
Put it down over *there*.

The word ***their*** means 'belonging to them'.

They like *their* home comforts.
Their friends are rather strange.

The word ***they're*** is the short form of *they* ***a****re*. The apostrophe is in place of the missing letter ***a***.

They're late.
The teachers said *they're* coming at 9pm.

> **Tip:** It may help you to remember that *t**here*** goes with ***here*** in meaning and spelling.

Now test yourself

Put *they're*, *their* or *there* in the gap to complete each sentence. You can check your answers on page 223.

1 ______ aren't any chocolates left.

2 ______ are six doughnuts on the plate.

3 ______ decision not to come seems odd.

4 They live in London, but ______ parents live in Devon.

5 I'm not sure why ______ not here yet.

6 ______ were many articles about it in the press.

7 ______ going to buy a new PC.

8 He says ______ car is too old to fix.

through / though / threw

These are three different words. ***Through*** and ***threw*** sound the same although their meanings are different. Make sure you don't write one when you mean one of the others.

The word ***through*** means 'from end to end, or side to side' or 'by way of' or 'by means of'.

To get to Reading we went *through* Newbury.
They stuck to each other *through* thick and thin.

The word ***though*** means 'even if' or 'although'.

Though he's tired, he'll manage to get there tonight.
They'll do it *though* they won't be very happy about it.

The word ***threw*** is a form of the verb *throw*.

He *threw* the ball from the boundary and hit the stumps.
She *threw* a party for her father's 80th birthday.

> **Tip:** It may help you to remember that *th**r**e**w*** comes from the verb *th**r**o**w*** and so both have an ***r*** and a **w**.

Now test yourself

Put *through*, *though* or *threw* in the gap to complete each sentence. You can check your answers on pages 223–4.

1 They ______ their old sofa out.

2 I dropped the ball even ______ he ______ it to me gently.

3 They'll go ______ the motions but they won't actually do anything.

4 They are determined to stay together ______ thick and thin.

5 ______ he's short he can still reach the shelf.

6 They ran______the tunnel at top speed.

7 He ______ the ball into the crowd.

8 The programme plays music ______ the night.

too / to / two

These are three different words but they sound exactly the same. Make sure you don't write one when you mean one of the others.

The word ***too*** means 'more than is needed or suitable' and 'also'.

He helped himself to far *too* much cream.
It's *too* hot to do anything.
That costs *too* much.
I'd like to come *too*. Is that OK?

The word ***to*** is often used in front of a verb and also when talking about going towards something.

I want *to* go home.
They gave the cup *to* the team captain.
It's ten minutes *to* two.
They are going *to* Paris for the weekend.

The word ***two*** is the number that follows one, the total of one plus one.

They have *two* boys.
There are *two* ways to get there.
He'll eat *two* slices of toast.

Now test yourself

Put *to*, *too* or *two* in the gap to complete each sentence. You can check your answers on page 224.

1 I'm going ______ help him tomorrow.

2 They can't fit in the car ______.

3 There are ______ many people coming to the party.

4 How many glasses are there on the table? ______.

5 ______ get to London by 10 o'clock you need ______ take the 8.50 train.

6 He was ______ hasty so he missed the most important clues.

7 Why doesn't she buy one ______? They're such a bargain.

8 It's______late. The train's already left.

where / we're / were / wear

These are four different words. ***Where*** and ***wear*** may sound the same but have completely different meanings. The other two, ***we're*** and ***were***, sound similar. Make sure you don't write one when you mean one of the others.

The word ***where*** is a word that relates to place. It can be a question word or link two parts of a sentence.

Where did you leave the papers?
He doesn't know *where* he's going.

The word ***we're*** is short for 'we are'. The apostrophe stands for the letter ***a***.

We're going to be late.
They asked us where *we're* eating tonight.

The word **were** is a form of the verb *be* used when talking about the past.

When they stayed with us they *were* very unhappy.
The children *were* very excited.

The word ***wear*** means 'to be dressed in'.

What shall I *wear* tomorrow?
You'll need to *wear* something casual.

Tip: It may help you to remember that w***here*** goes with ***here*** in meaning and spelling.

Now test yourself

Put *wear*, *where*, *were* or *we're* in the gap to complete each sentence. You can check your answers on page 224.

1 They lived ______ they could find work.

2 ______ too old to retrain.

3 ______ whatever you like to the party.

4 ______ is my diary?

5 ______ very happy to see you!

6 Why ______ they standing in front of the screen?

who's / whose

These are two different words, but they sound the same. Make sure you don't write one when you mean the other.

The word ***who's*** is short for 'who is' or 'who has'.

> Guess *who's* coming to dinner.
> *Who's* making all that noise?
> *Who's* done this?

The word ***whose*** can indicate 'belonging to a person'. It can also be a question word.

> He's the man *whose* wife left him.
> *Whose* fault is it?

Tip: Remember that the apostrophe is used to show a missing letter or letters.

Now test yourself

Put either *who's* or *whose* in the gap to complete each sentence. You can check your answers on page 225.

1 He's the boy ______ mum works at the hospital.

2 ______ books are those?

3 ______ decision will that be?

4 ______ coming to the meeting?

5 ______ finished their work?

6 That's the manager ______ team got the special award.

7 Can you tell me ______ jacket you like best?

8 Do you know ______ on the interview panel?

9 'Those aren't my books.' '______ are they then?'

10 Why can't you tell me ______ money it is?

PART D

HOW TO SET ABOUT WRITING SOMETHING ... ANYTHING ... EVERYTHING

The PROCESS method

The purpose of this section of the book is to give you a method you can use whenever you have to write something. I'll call this method the PROCESS method, and you can use the letters of the word PROCESS to help you remember the different things that it involves.

I will start by looking at the letters P, C and S in the word ProCeSs. These stand for:

- purpose
- content
- structure

The purpose

Whatever it is that you want to write, the first thing you should think about is your **purpose**. Ask yourself: '**Why** do I need to write this?'

The answer might be:

- I want the bank manager to know about the mistake the bank has made and to put it right.
- I need to pass information to my colleague about my morning's work.
- I want my son's teacher to check my son's breathing after PE classes.
- I want to thank my friend for such a lovely evening.
- I want that job!

By looking at these examples we can see that *the person we are writing to* is closely linked to why we are writing. So a second question to ask yourself is: '**Who** am I writing to?'

We have seen some possible answers in the list above:

- the bank manager
- a colleague
- my son's teacher
- my friend
- a potential employer

You can probably think of many other people you might write to.

Keeping in mind the person we are writing to can help us decide:

- which points to include
- which points to leave out
- what sort of language we should use

For example, one task might be to write an e-mail to someone you know well to ask them to send you a booklet. This doesn't have to be a long message, but it still needs to be polite:

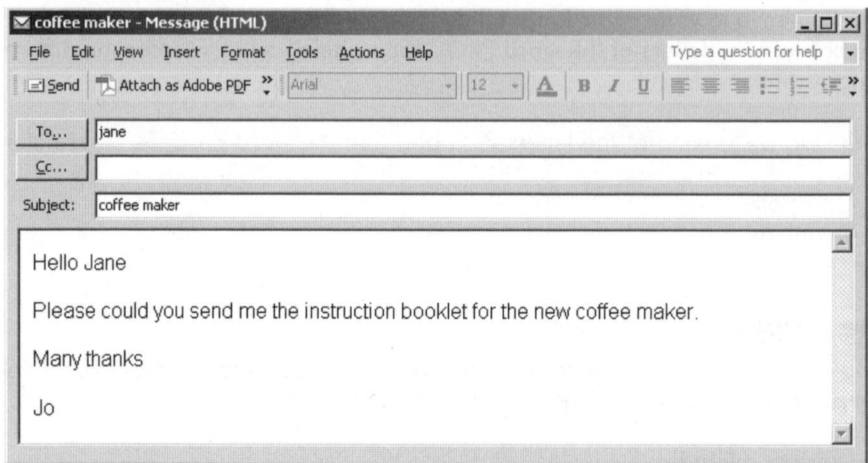

But if you have to write an e-mail to someone you don't know – perhaps someone in another department or another organization – you may need to write in a slightly different way and provide more of an explanation:

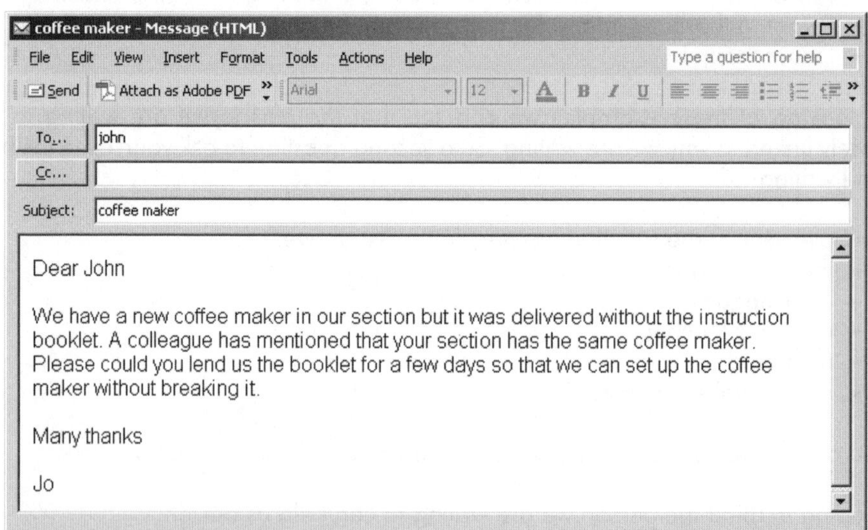

coffee maker - Message (HTML)
File Edit View Insert Format Tools Actions Help
Type a question for help
Send Attach as Adobe PDF
Arial
12
To... john
Cc...
Subject: coffee maker
Dear John
We have a new coffee maker in our section but it was delivered without the instruction booklet. A colleague has mentioned that your section has the same coffee maker. Please could you lend us the booklet for a few days so that we can set up the coffee maker without breaking it.
Many thanks
Jo

What do I want to achieve?

While we are thinking about the **purpose** of what we're writing, we need to ask ourselves a third question: '**What** do I want this piece of writing to achieve?'

Or we might put this another way: 'What do I want the reader to do when they have read it?'

The answer might be:

- to send me what I've asked for
- to phone me
- to make sure my child is OK after PE classes
- to offer me an interview

Here are six things you might need to write. What is the purpose of these documents?

- a note to the milkman
- an e-mail to the seller of an item on eBay
- a note to a teacher at school after your child has been off school for a week
- a letter to your bank manager
- a section on your appraisal form at work about training needs
- a report for your manager to give your recommendations for improving productivity

Here are my suggestions. Notice that there could be more than one purpose in some cases – you may have thought of other reasons for writing.

document	***purpose***
a note to the milkman	to ensure the milkman delivers what you need on the right day
an e-mail to the seller of an item on eBay	to get more information about the item
a note to a teacher at school after your child has been off school for a week	to ensure the absence is properly recorded in the register and it is clear your child was not playing truant
a letter to your bank manager	to request an extension to your overdraft; to ask for compensation for the bank's error
a section on your appraisal form at work about training needs	to get you the right training to do your job better; to help you get the promotion you want
a report for your manager to give your recommendations for improving productivity	to get the work done more effectively; to show your manager you're thinking constructively about the work the team does

If you have a clear idea about what you are trying to achieve, you should find that the task of finding the right words is much easier.

Checklist

- Always think about your purpose.
- First ask yourself, 'Why do I need to write this?'
- Then ask yourself, 'Who am I writing to?'
- Then ask yourself, 'What do I want the reader to do when they have read it?'

The content

Just keeping the answers to the questions 'Why am I writing this?', 'Who am I writing to?' and 'What do I want to achieve?' fixed in your mind will help you to work out the **content** – what you need to include in the document.

Readers quickly lose interest when they try to read a document that includes a lot of irrelevant points – things they don't need to know. So to keep your readers focused on your message, you need to include only the relevant points – the things they really do need to know. Writers sometimes seem to think they need to make the document long for people to think it's important. Readers disagree. So when you're writing, stick to the points you need to make.

Let's go back to the e-mail asking for the coffee-maker instructions. It could have been written like this:

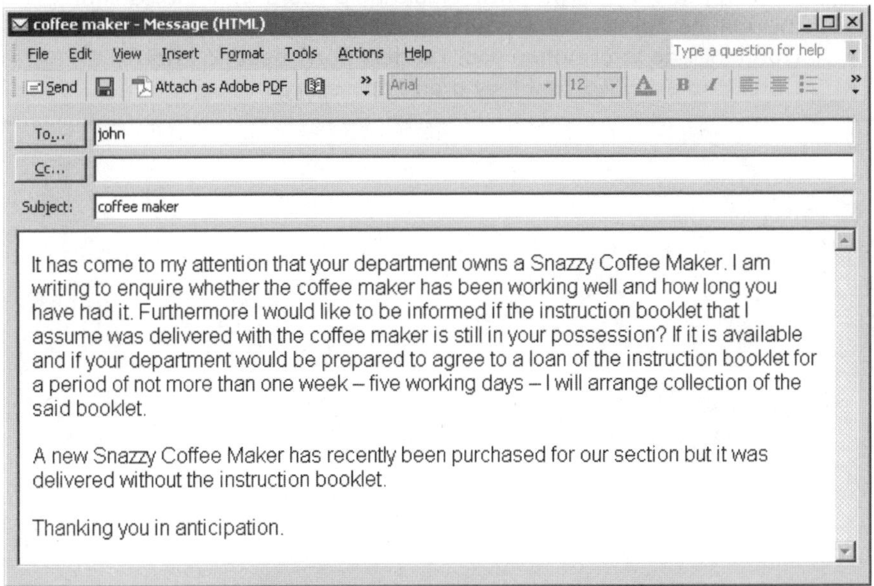

coffee maker - Message (HTML)

To... john

Cc...

Subject: coffee maker

It has come to my attention that your department owns a Snazzy Coffee Maker. I am writing to enquire whether the coffee maker has been working well and how long you have had it. Furthermore I would like to be informed if the instruction booklet that I assume was delivered with the coffee maker is still in your possession? If it is available and if your department would be prepared to agree to a loan of the instruction booklet for a period of not more than one week – five working days – I will arrange collection of the said booklet.

A new Snazzy Coffee Maker has recently been purchased for our section but it was delivered without the instruction booklet.

Thanking you in anticipation.

This is rather longer than the version on page 122. The grammar is correct but it's not a good e-mail – it has too many words and it sounds rather pompous.

There are several reasons for this:

- Some of the extra words add new – but unnecessary – points. For example, think about the words *I am writing to inquire whether the coffee maker has been working well and how long you have had it*. This is not the reason for the e-mail – and the query about how long the colleague has had it is just pointless padding.
- Some of the extra words are just waffle: the old trick of using 20 words

when 10 will do. Readers get bored easily and when they're bored they tend to stop reading. We should try to make our points in as few words as possible, while still being polite. For example, *I would like to be informed* could be written *Please tell me;* and *If your department would be prepared to agree to a loan of the instruction booklet for a period of not more than one week* could be just as polite if you wrote *Please could you lend me the booklet for a week.*

This e-mail could have been so much shorter, and so much less boring. The risk of an overlong message is that the reader won't be able to see what they're being asked to do ... so they won't do it.

Checklist

- Thinking about your purpose should help you decide the content.
- Include the points your readers need to know.
- Don't include information your readers don't need to know.
- Don't add extra words if they aren't necessary.

The structure

When you have sorted out the purpose and the content of your document, you need to work on the **structure**. This part of writing is all about:

- putting the points we want to make in the best order
- showing that order as clearly as possible to the reader

Putting the points in the best order

The same letter or note could appear with a number of structures – but how do we decide which is the best?

Let's take the example of a dad writing to the school to ask the teacher to check his child after sports classes.

Take a look at this letter. Imagine you are a teacher at a primary school about to take the register for 30 enthusiastic 7-year-olds. How easy would it be for you to see what this letter is about?

> *Dear Miss Khan*
>
> *I've had to take Tim to the doctor's several times recently because of his breathing. He's been coughing too. I was worried about him and wanted to know if it was alright for him to continue to play sport at school – he really loves his rounders. The doctor has recommended he continues sport but wants us to keep a close check on his breathing after each playtime and sports lesson. He says all I need to do is take his pulse and time his breathing. More than 20 breaths per minute would suggest he's having difficulty. The doctor also said Tim could check his own breathing but he felt it would be useful to have an adult – us or a teacher – check what he finds. And the doctor pointed out that if he was really short of breath he probably wouldn't be able to do it himself very accurately. Could you help with this, please. Tim would need to be checked at the end of every playtime and PE class.*

This letter would take quite a while to read, and your child's teacher would probably thank you if you could make the message easier to grasp.

So what's wrong with the letter? We can use the PROCESS method – Purpose, Content and Structure – to assess how well it works:

- The **purpose** is unclear until the very end of the letter, when you see the words *Could you help with this, please*.
- The **content** includes too many points that are not relevant to the purpose of the letter.
- There are at least three things wrong with the **structure**: the key point is not obvious at first glance, so the reader must read all the text that's there; there's no indication to the reader what the letter's about; and the text is a single block that looks unfriendly to the reader.

This letter contains lots of information that doesn't need to be there, especially at the beginning of the letter. What is there may be true, and it may be very important to the parent. But because it is there, the teacher can't see the point of the letter as quickly as she needs to.

So here is a good rule for the structure of any note, letter, or e-mail: **put the key points first**. The sooner your reader can see what your letter is about – and why they need to read it – the better.

Another reason for putting the key points first and leaving the detail until later is that people often don't read to the end of a letter. If you put key points in the final paragraph, without drawing the reader's attention to them, they might not be read.

Think of how you react yourself when you have to read something. When we are reading we don't always read to the end of every letter or e-mail we receive. So as writers we must be careful not to hide anything we particularly need our reader to see (or do!) in a paragraph near the middle or the end of the letter.

Showing the order to the reader

There are some other useful rules about structure that will become obvious if you look at the two letters below. Compare them and ask yourself which you'd rather read.

Dear Miss Khan

Please could you help us monitor Tim's breathing after sport activities in class and at playtime. He's been having difficulties recently – getting out of breath – and the doctor has suggested we monitor his breathing closely. I attach a form to record the results – it explains exactly what to do. Please confirm you are able to do this – Tim understands what's needed so he should help. If you have any questions or problems with this, please phone me on 12345 12234565 or see me in the playground.

Many thanks

Dear Miss Khan

<u>Breathing check for Tim Brown after playtime and sport classes</u>

Please could you help us monitor Tim's breathing after sport activities in class and at playtime. He's been having difficulties recently – getting out of breath – and the doctor has suggested we monitor his breathing closely.

I attach a form to record the results – it explains exactly what to do. Please confirm you are able to do this – Tim understands what's needed so he should help. If you have any questions or problems with this, please phone me on 12345 12234565 or see me in the playground.

Many thanks

Which letter would you prefer to read? So which letter would the teacher prefer to read?

You probably noticed that the wording is the same in each. But the second letter is so much easier to read. The differences are in:

- the use of spacing
- the use of a heading

One obvious difference is that the first example is presented as one long paragraph. The second example breaks the writing up into two shorter paragraphs. This means there is more white space and the letter is easier to read.

The other obvious difference is that in the first example you can't see at a glance what the letter is about. The important information is there, but you need to read the letter to find what's being asked for. But in the second letter the heading tells us straight away what the letter is about.

The two letters are organized in the same way – the points come in the same order in each – but that extra white space and the well-chosen heading in bold type make all the difference.

So here is our second rule about structure: **never underestimate how important the look of a document is**. This is true for typed and handwritten documents, for e-mails, letters, notes and reports.

Readers unanimously prefer to look at documents with:

- plenty of white space
- paragraphs of a manageable length
- helpful headings and subheadings

More about structure

I want to look at some more examples of how taking the trouble to make the structure clear can be helpful to your readers.

The documents on pages 131 and 132 show two different ways that a memo from the Human Resources department to everyone in the organization could be written.

Put yourself in the position of a reader. Ask yourself:

- Do I want to read this? Would I read it if I didn't have to?
- How easily can I see what it's about?
- How quickly can I go back over the text and check the details of some points?

Notice to Employees
March 2006

We've made some important decisions recently about the way we work. We're planning to put these ideas into practice over the next few weeks. You will now be able to choose when you do your hours. You'll have complete freedom to work when you want. We recognize that people work better when they eat healthy food so our canteen will produce only recipes approved by top TV chef Ollie Pucker – nutritious, healthy and delicious. The canteen will be free for all employees and will be open from 7am to 8pm. Membership for our on-site gymnasium and pool will now be free – we're hoping that employees will take up this offer of free fitness. We are revising our holiday policy: all employees will be entitled to 40 days of annual leave plus the statutory bank holidays. Holiday not taken one year can be taken the following year. And finally our health care plan is now extended to cover all members of your family: this includes spouse, children, parents and your brothers and sisters. You can have an annual health check and immediate access to traditional and alternative therapies. A recent study of the causes of days lost through illness has shown many people are off work because of backache. To help reduce this, we have engaged a specialist to check that the chairs and desks in the offices are right for each employee, a masseur to reduce tension in neck and shoulder blades, and a physiotherapist to show employees how to sit at their desks in the way that will best help their backs. Please take advantage of all these benefits. We hope they will make you even happier than you are already!

Changing your working life – for the better

We've made some important decisions recently about the way we work. We're planning to put these ideas into practice over the next few weeks.

Complete flexitime
You will now be able to choose when you do your hours. You'll have complete freedom to work when you want.

Nutritious and delicious food in the canteen – free
We recognize that people work better when they eat healthy food so our canteen will produce only recipes approved by top TV chef Ollie Pucker – nutritious, healthy and delicious. The canteen will be free for all employees and will be open from 7am to 8pm.

Free gym membership for you and your family
Membership for our on-site gymnasium and pool will now be free – we're hoping that employees will take up this offer of free fitness.

40 days of annual leave for all
We are revising our holiday policy: all employees will be entitled to 40 days of annual leave plus the statutory bank holidays. Holiday not taken one year can be taken the following year.

Free health care extended to your family
Our health care plan is now extended to cover all members of your family: this includes spouse, children, parents and your brothers and sisters. You can have an annual health check and immediate access to traditional and alternative therapies.

Special help for bad back sufferers
A recent study of the causes of days lost through illness has shown many people are off work because of backache. To help reduce this, we have engaged a specialist to check that the chairs and desks in the offices are right for each employee, a masseur to reduce tension in neck and shoulder blades, and a physiotherapist to show employees how to sit at their desks in the way that will best help their backs.

Please take advantage of all these benefits. We hope they will make you even happier than you are already!

Human Resources Team
March 2006

Which would you prefer to read? We can use the PROCESS method – Purpose, Content and Structure – to assess how well each works:

- The **purpose** of the first version is not clear until you start reading; but in the second version the purpose is stated in the heading and this leads the reader into the document.
- The first version of the document looks so unwelcoming that you might never find out about the **content** because you don't even start to read it; but in the second version the subheadings make it easy to see what the main points are.
- The first version has a well-organized **structure** (the text is the same as the second document) but the heading is more likely to discourage people from reading than draw them into the document; but in the second version it is easy to see the structure.

Let's consider another example. Imagine you've recently offered to help with a social event, and the organizer has sent you a note about what you have to do.

> Dear Knut,
> Many thanks for offering to help organize the party. I've planned what needs to be done. Here are the things I'd like you to sort: booking the band – we'd like them to start around 9 and perform for a total of two hours – it'll be fine if they want to break this up into two or three sets because we have the venue all night; can you arrange enough bar staff for the night – they'll need to be on site from 6pm until the bar closes at 2am; check with the caterers that they have included vegetarian and vegan food as well as things for meat eaters; they should cater for about 250 people and reckon on at least 50 being vegetarian, probably 20 vegans. I've tried to get more precise numbers for this but no success, so far – we'll have to go with these figures; check decorations in the main hall have been ordered: Sasha Govan is in charge of that; get a copy of the security staff list – who'll be on duty that night and their mobile numbers.
> Thanks a million – let me know if any of these prove tricky and I'll help.

Dear Knut,

Many thanks for offering to help organize the party. I've planned what needs to be done. Here are the things I'd like you to sort:

- **Book the band** – we'd like them to start around 9 and perform for two hours. They can break this up into two or three sets – we have the venue all night.
- **Arrange enough bar staff** to cover from 6pm until the bar closes at 2am.
- **Check the caterers** will provide food for about 250 people: 50 vegetarian, and probably 20 vegans. This is my best guess.
- **Check with Sasha Govan** that decorations in the main hall have been ordered.
- **Find out which security staff** will be on duty that night and what their mobile numbers are.

Thanks a million – let me know if any of these prove tricky and I'll help.

Look at the two versions and ask yourself:

- Do I want to read this? Would I read it if I didn't have to?
- How easily can I see what it's about?
- How quickly can I go back over the text and check the details of some points?

When you've decided which version of the note you'd rather read and work from, ask yourself why that is.

Did you prefer the second version of the note? That's the one preferred by everyone I asked! Some of the reasons people gave for preferring this version were:

- **Bullet points** make it easy to see the different tasks – and to check them off the list when you've done them.
- **The use of bold** picks out the key idea from each bullet point. It isn't so easy to achieve bold when writing by hand – but you can use underlining or a coloured pen to achieve the same effect.
- **White space** around each point helps focus your eyes on the text.

- **Only relevant points** are included.
- **A verb** at the beginning of each instruction makes it easy to see what you need to do.
- **Fewer words** are used to cover the points.

Headings

Headings can be a useful way of stressing what the main point is and making the structure clear. This can be a great help to all of us.

When we read a letter or an e-mail, a heading can help prepare us for what's coming. That means that as we start reading we already know why we're reading and so we're ready to take on board any new information. And when we're writing, the act of putting a heading on our letters forces us to think carefully about what our main point is. So it's worth spending some time picking the best heading for a letter or e-mail – one that tells the reader as much as possible about what's to follow.

Read each of these headings and imagine what would follow in the letter. Would the heading help you to see why you needed to read the letter, and so to start reading it?

Playtime
Pay
Trip

I expect you'll agree that these headings give you only a vague idea what the letter is about.

How about these headings? Do they give you a better idea what the letter will be about?

Bullying at playtime
Pay cuts reviewed
Trip to the zoo

These headings would help you to see why you needed to read the letter, but it is possible to choose headings that would be even more helpful:

How we make sure children are not bullied at playtime
Pay cuts reversed
Day trip to the zoo: 20 June

Subheadings

The main heading on a document gives the general idea of what the letter or e-mail is about. But you can also use subheadings inside it. Subheadings help the reader to:

- read the structure of the document at a glance
- find more information about a particular point quickly

Even if you provide a helpful main heading, the reader may still have to work through the writing that follows. Subheadings can allow the reader to see straight away how you've divided up the topic. For example, if you are writing a letter about a school trip, you might group the information about the trip under subheadings like these:

Aim of the trip
How you can help
How to volunteer

We have already seen on page 133 how useful subheadings can be in making it easy to read a piece of writing.

Checklist

- Put the key points first so the reader doesn't miss them.
- Never underestimate how important the look of a document is. Readers like documents with short paragraphs and plenty of white space.
- Use headings and subheadings to make the structure clear.

Planning before you write

Our key words from the PROCESS method so far are **purpose**, **content** and **structure**. I've introduced them in that order because that's the order we should think about them in before we start to write.

So far I've used those headings to talk about the things you need to think about to produce a good document. We're now going to work through a method to help you achieve this.

Think for a moment about how you go about writing something. One or more of these comments might match what you do:

- 'I worry about it for a while, put it off and then spend time thinking about ways of not doing it at all or getting someone else to do it.'
- 'I like to get straight down to it – I use my computer and type it all out. Then I read through what I've got and make any changes. Sometimes I find this is the bit that takes the longest. I may have to delete some sections, add in new points, and sometimes move chunks of text around using Cut and Paste. When I'm happy with it I print it out and send it off immediately before I change my mind again.'
- 'Mostly I write what I need to write by hand. I tend to do a rough copy first. I edit that – sometimes I need to re-write completely. The final stage is writing it up neatly.'
- 'Whatever I need to write, it always takes so much longer than I think it should.'

Of course there is no single way to write. Not all the things we write need to be planned carefully before we put pen to paper. But working from a plan is the best way to approach most writing tasks.

Many people groan at the idea of having to write a plan. They tell me that writing a plan will mean an extra stage in the writing process. That is true. But the time taken to write that plan can usually be saved later on in the writing process. It should take less time to write the document itself. If the plan is a good one, the first draft will be pretty close to the final draft, and certainly closer than something bashed out on a keyboard without a plan.

Having a plan gives you several benefits:

- It forces you to work out your ideas **before** you start to write.
- It says **what points** you want to make and **the best order** for them.
- It frees you to **focus on the words and phrases you choose** to put your ideas across.

If you don't have to worry about getting the content and the structure right, then what you write first time round stands a better chance of being grammatically correct and clearly expressed. But if you try to work out what you need to say at the same time as you write, what you produce is often not quite right. You may have included too many points, missed some out, and got some of your points in the wrong order. Fixing this takes time. Even if you are working on a computer and can drag text around or use 'Cut and Paste', it is still easy to make mistakes, and it still takes time.

I hope you're convinced. Try it out.

A five-stage plan

Here's a method that is easy to use and reflects the way our brain works. It separates the tasks – what to include and what order to put the points in – and lets our brain think stage by stage.

Stage 1 of the process involves thinking about your **purpose**. Ask yourself:

- Who am I writing to?
- What do I want them to do when they've read my letter, e-mail or note?

Keep the answers to these two questions in mind as you move on to stage 2.

Stage 2 of the process involves thinking about your **content**. Think about your purpose and ask yourself what you need to write to achieve your purpose. On a blank piece of paper write one or two words to represent each point you come up with and draw a circle around each, so that it looks like a bubble or a balloon.

Don't worry about the order of your points at this stage. Trying get the order right immediately makes it more difficult for our brain to produce something. It is much easier if you note down all the important points without worrying where they should go.

Your paper should end up looking something like this, except that your bubbles will have something written inside them:

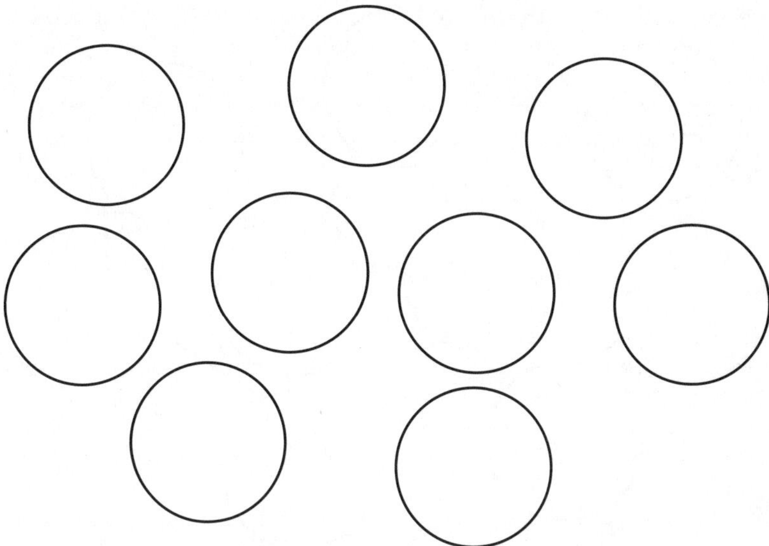

Once you have got all your points down, pause, stand back, and take another look at what you have written.

Now reconsider the purpose of your letter and who you are writing to. Ask yourself whether all those points are necessary, and cross out any unnecessary points.

Stage 3 of the process involves drawing lines between the bubbles to link points that are related to each other and which you will deal with together.

The points you link together at this stage might well be dealt with together in paragraphs in your final document.

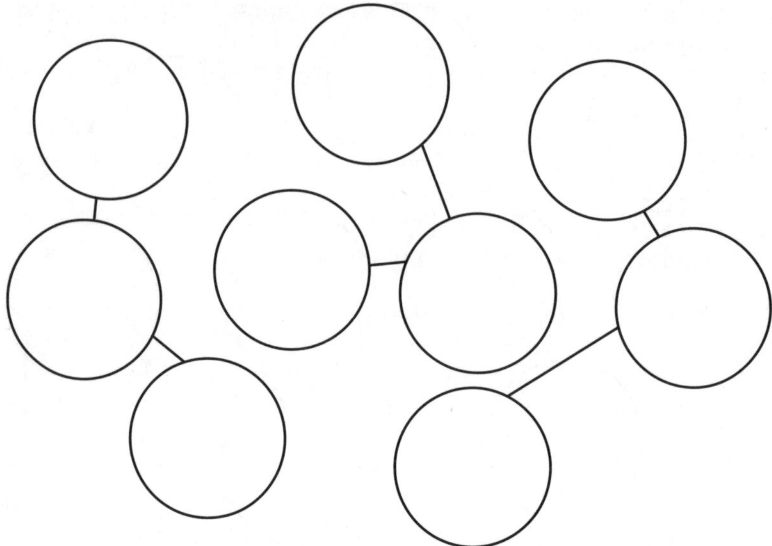

Stage 4 of the process involves numbering your points in the order you want to write about them. Remember that you should put the key points first to make sure that the reader knows what you are writing about. You should also make sure that points that are linked to each other are dealt with at the same time and not in different parts of your document.

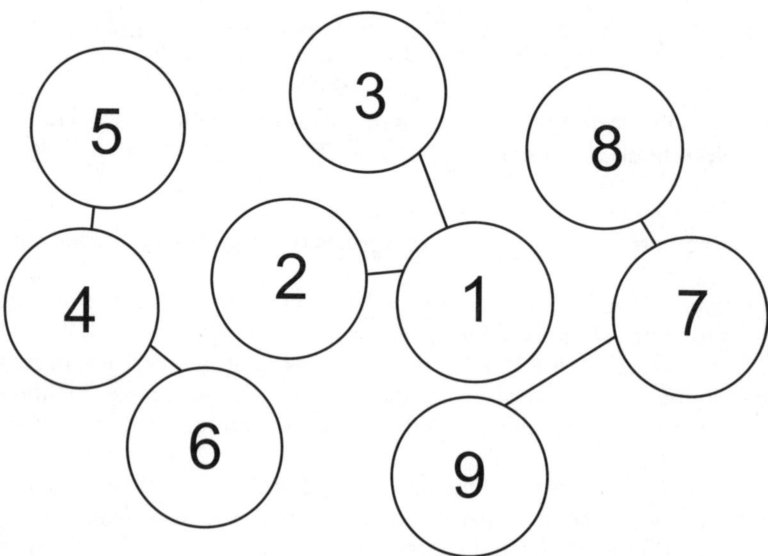

Stage 5 of the process involves putting your plan to one side for a while before you take another look at it later. Putting this distance between you and the document helps you to be more objective about how good what you've done is.

When you come back to your plan with a clear head, check it meets the purpose of the letter:

- Have you included the right points – not too many, and not too few?
- Are the points arranged in the right order?

At this stage, depending on what you're writing, who it's for and how important it is, you may like to show your plan to a friend, or a colleague, maybe to your boss or the person who asked you to write the letter. If they confirm that your plan is good, you should be able to approach the next stage, writing the document, with confidence: you know what you need to include and what order to put the points in. All you need to think about are the best words and phrases to express your message clearly.

When you are ready to start writing, you can use your diagram to guide you:

- Start at bubble number 1.
- Work out the best way to put that point into words.
- Write it down.
- Put a tick through that bubble.
- Move on to the next bubble and repeat the process.

Practice exercise: Planning

Now use this technique to plan a letter. This is the situation:

- You live in a town that has had a parking permit system since 1997. The street you live in has parking down one side, but houses without driveways down both sides, so parking is always tight.
- Every household in the street is entitled to two parking permits. At the moment the permits cover 8am to 6pm; outside those hours anyone can park in the road.
- The street is near the town centre so there are restaurants and bars nearby. Much to the frustration of the majority of people in your street, if you try to park your car in the street around 6pm or later, it's virtually impossible. Early in the evening, spaces are taken up by people who work in the nearby restaurants; later in the evening it's people going out in town who park there.
- Someone in the street said they'd write to the Council asking for the hours of the permit to be extended until 10pm instead of 6pm. This would mean people from the street had a better chance of parking close to home. Everyone in the street thought this was a great idea and willingly signed a petition. But the letter hasn't been sent (or written) yet. You've

decided to write it to try to get everything moving: you're fed up carrying your shopping to your front door from 500 yards away.

Let's go through the stages we talked about.

For **stage 1**, we must think about our purpose. We are writing to the local council's parking permit section, and our purpose is to get them to extend our parking permits from 6pm to 10pm, or at least to let us know what we need to do.

For **stage 2**, we need to think about the content. Jot down what you think you need to include in the letter. Ask yourself what you need to include in order to achieve your purpose.

Once you've got your points down you need to check whether all the points are necessary.

Look at your own bubble diagram and weed out anything that doesn't need to be there. Then check you really have included all the points that need to be in the letter.

Now take a look at my bubble diagram. What would you add or get rid of?

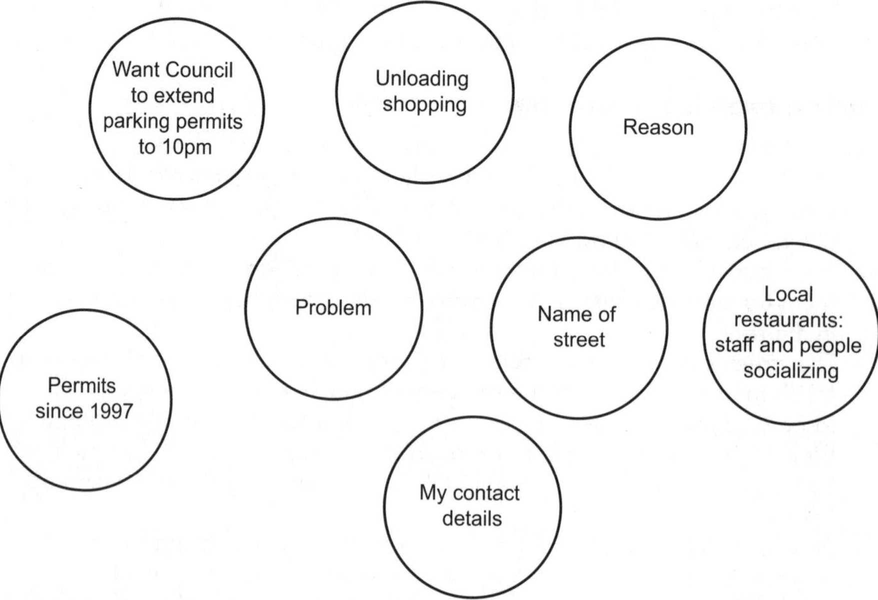

I would get rid of one bubble: *Permits since 1997*. It is true, but it has no place in the letter. The Council knows this fact and I know it, but it won't affect whether the Council can extend the permit times.

I would add one extra point about the petition. I intend to enclose it with my letter so I need to mention it in the letter. The petition may help me achieve my purpose because the Council will be more likely to listen to a request from all the residents in a street than from a single household.

For **stage 3**, draw lines between the bubbles to link points that are related to each other.

For **stage 4**, number the points. Remember you want to put the **key points first** in the letter. The key points here are the street I'm talking about and what I want to happen.

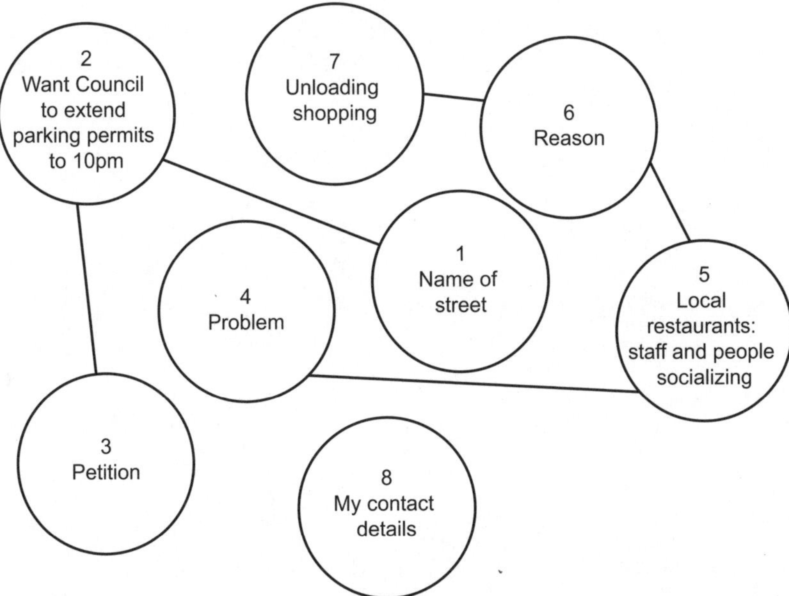

For **stage 5**, we're going to put our plan to one side for the moment. It's always a good idea to do this to enable you to check later whether what you've included is right and that it's all in the right order. If you do this as soon as you've finished the plan, you won't give yourself a chance to have second thoughts.

We'll come back to this practice exercise on page 154, but for the time being we can be happy that we have used our five-stage process to create a plan, and that our plan will make it easy for us to write the letter and to achieve our purpose.

Checklist

- Writing is usually easier if you have a plan.
- Use these five stages to make a plan: 1. Think about your purpose. 2. Jot down what you need to include. 3. Draw lines to link related points. 4. Number your points. 5. Take a break before coming back to your plan with a clear head.

Style

While we put our plan to one side for a moment, I want to take the opportunity to think about the next part of the PROCESS method. So far we have talked about:

Purpose
R
O
Content
E
Structure
S

The final S stands for the **style** we want to use in our writing. By the word 'style' I mean the particular words and phrases we use to express our ideas.

We need to be sure what we write is clear and easy to understand. How do we achieve this?

Let's begin from the point of view of the reader. What don't you like reading? Think about any documents you have seen recently that you found difficult to read. Can you remember them in enough detail to jot down what made them hard going?

Perhaps your reasons included some of these points:

- It contained a lot of mistakes that made it difficult to understand.
- It used a lot of long words and words I didn't understand.
- It was too long.
- The sentences seemed to go on forever.

We know what sort of things we don't like to read, so we know what we should try to avoid as writers.

Use correct grammar and good punctuation

We've already looked at the key points of grammar and punctuation in Parts A and B of this book.

Accurate spelling and correct grammar are important when we write. If we make a grammatical mistake or get the punctuation wrong readers may misunderstand us, or they may think that we haven't taken much care over what we've written, or they may think we simply don't know what's correct.

If they think we don't know how to write correctly they may also – and maybe unfairly – decide that we don't know what we're writing about either. So we are less likely to achieve our purpose.

Use everyday words

Most of us don't like reading things that contain lots of unnecessarily long words. Many people imagine that using long words is a sign of good writing – perhaps because when we were at school our teachers encouraged us to try to use long words to show we had learnt how to use them. But most of the writing we do in our adult life is to pass on information. The best way to do this is to choose words that our readers will understand easily. If an everyday word says what we want to say, then it's the best word to choose.

Quick check

Mask the answers with your hand or a piece of paper. Can you think of simpler alternatives for these words? Unmask the text and check your answers.

1 assistance

help

2 cease

stop

3 commence

start, begin

4 endeavour

attempt, try

5 prior to

before

6 utilize

use

Choose verbs to express actions

Using everyday language need not just apply to your choice of words. It can also apply to the way you shape your sentences.

People sometimes think they need to be more formal when they write. We can see that in the choice of words they use. For example, they might say *if your car breaks down*, but they might write *in the event of vehicular breakdown*.

The key change here is that the more formal sentence has used the noun *breakdown* rather than the verb *breaks down*. This might help it sound rather grand, but when we write our main aim is usually to convey information. Keeping the verb rather than the noun to express the action – as we do naturally when we speak – has two great advantages:

- We use fewer words.
- Our writing sounds crisper.

(If you're not sure what a verb is, check pages 12–21.)

Quick check

Mask the answers with your hand or a piece of paper. Make these sentences shorter and crisper by expressing the action with a verb. Unmask the text and check your answers.

1 They arranged the provision of tea and coffee for the meeting.
They arranged to provide tea and coffee for the meeting.

2 They made reference to the letter he had sent them.
They referred to the letter he had sent them.

3 She quickly came to the conclusion that they had made a mistake.
She quickly concluded that they had made a mistake.

Now test yourself

Try to make these sentences shorter and crisper by using a verb rather than a noun to express the action. You can check your answers on page 226.

1 Lynne made the assumption that they'd be on time.

2 His expectation was that they would help.

3 The committee found it hard to come to the decision.

4 They reached the completion of the roadworks in July.

5 They made an investigation into the accusations.

6 The school has made arrangements for the children to attend the concert.

7 They wanted to hold a discussion about the problem.

8 The team has made an announcement about the new start date.

Use as few words as possible

As we write we should focus on finding the clearest and the shortest way to express the points we want to make. Sometimes writers have the idea that a longer document will impress more than a shorter document. But I've never met anyone who would prefer the long version of a document, rather than the short version. As readers we want to read and get on with the next thing – as writers we need to remember this!

Quick check

Mask the answers with your hand or a piece of paper. Rewrite these sentences using everyday words and get rid of any words that don't need to be there. Unmask the text and check your answers.

1 I would be most grateful if you could assist me with the preparation of coffee after the meeting.

Please help me prepare the coffee after the meeting.

2 Failure to notify the committee of your intention to cease preparation of the hall for meetings has been the cause of much inconvenience.

You didn't tell the committee you weren't going to continue to prepare the hall for meetings and this has been very inconvenient.

3 In the event of severe weather conditions the event will be postponed by the committee.

The committee will postpone the event if the weather's bad.

4 Your child is required to take a swimming costume and towel to school on Fridays.

Your child will need to bring a towel and swimming costume on Fridays.

5 Prior to the commencement of the concert, wine will be offered to the audience.

Before the concert begins, we'll serve wine.

Keep your sentences short

Sentences that run on and on can make writing really difficult to read. Would you like to have to read this sentence?

> As long as the condition of the cinema has improved before the film is shown at the first Saturday afternoon performance during the festival, most people will be satisfied that what the judges decided before the festival started was

definitely the right way to go about assessing such a difficult problem and coming to a workable solution.

This sentence is grammatically correct, and it is certainly not the longest sentence I've ever read. But as we read, it doesn't take us long to realize we don't have enough full stops. Without full stops we have no real place to pause. And without a proper pause, we cannot digest what we are reading.

Experts agree that if we can keep our average sentence length to **15–20 words**, we are well on the way to producing readable writing. This does not mean you should treat 20 words as the maximum sentence length allowed – indeed, using the occasional longer sentence will help to keep your writing interesting. It's more a case of keeping an eye on sentence length and understanding that readers need to have information presented in manageable chunks.

Use one idea per sentence

One way to control sentence length is to recognize that a sentence should contain a single idea.

Take a look at this sentence:

> The new manager, who has been appointed by head office without any consultation with staff in the local office, has changed the contracts of 50% of the staff without consultation with the unions and drawn up a plan to make 20% redundant.

The sentence contains 43 words. That's going to make it difficult to read. But the sentence contains two different ideas, so I can break it down into two manageable sentences:

> The new manager has changed the contracts of 50% of the staff without consultation with the unions and drawn up a plan to make 20% redundant. He was appointed by head office without any consultation with staff in the local office.

I now have one sentence of 26 words and one of 15 words, which should be easier for readers to digest.

Now test yourself

Break these sentences into shorter sentences so that each contains one main idea. (Remember to aim for 15–20 words as an average sentence length.) You can check your answers on page 226.

1 The dentist was so exasperated by patients failing to pay for their treatment on time and booking appointments and not showing up that he decided to take drastic measures by not only refusing to see any patients who did this, but also removing them permanently from his list. (49 words)

2 While the minister claimed to agree in principle with the opinion expressed earlier that day by his colleague, he seemed unable to express that opinion clearly in his own words when quizzed about it by other politicians and the press. (41 words)

Use active verbs

For our final point about style, I want to return to the idea of how we use verbs. (If you're still not sure what a verb is, turn to pages 12–21.)

Take a look at this sentence:

> Should fresh towels be required by the children after the swimming gala, it is requested that these be made available to them at the changing room door by parents.

How does it sound to you? A little pompous or old-fashioned, perhaps?

Could we make it sound more like everyday language? What would you do to breathe a bit of life into the sentence? Have a go at rewriting it.

Here's what I came up with:

> If your child needs a fresh towel after the swimming gala, you should take one to the changing room door.

I hope you'll agree that this sounds more natural. The key difference between the sentences is in the verbs. Each verb now has a 'doer' in front of it: the 'doer' *your child* goes in front of *needs*, and the 'doer' *you* goes in front of *should take*. In grammatical terms the verbs have been changed from 'passive' verbs to 'active' verbs.

Active verbs generally mean that sentences are easier to understand. For you to use active verbs, all you need to do is check that you have a 'doer' before the verb in each sentence.

Quick check

Mask the answers with your hand or a piece of paper. In each sentence pick out the 'doer' and the verb that goes with it. Unmask the text and check your answers.

1 The boy kicked the ball.

doer: the boy; verb: kicked

2 John did the shopping.

doer: John; verb: did

3 His foot knocked the chair.

doer: his foot; verb: knocked

Avoid passive verbs if you can

Passive verbs make our writing sound formal and distant, and they sometimes mean that the reader misunderstands. If we write *The letter must be sent* there is a chance that no-one knows who has to send it; if we write *The decision was taken* we don't know who took the decision.

You *can* use passive verbs in your writing, but you should choose to use one for a particular reason. Passive verbs can be especially useful if you don't want to point the finger of blame. They allow you to say *The cup has been broken* without saying who broke it.

But in general, choose active verbs if you can. Active verbs will help you:

- write clearly, because you must include the doer
- write in a direct way, using the words *I* and *you* which create contact between reader and writer
- use fewer words
- write in an everyday, easy-to-understand style

Quick check

Mask the answers with your hand or a piece of paper. Rewrite these sentences using an active verb instead of a passive verb. Put the doer at the beginning of the sentence and you should automatically see what the active verb will be. Unmask the text and check your answers.

1 The book was published by More and Lang.
verb: was published; doer: More and Lang
More and Lang published the book.

2 The cake was abandoned in the garden by the boys.
verb: was abandoned; doer: the boys
The boys abandoned the cake in the garden.

3 The letters were sent by the school.
verb: were sent; doer: the school
The school sent the letters.

4 The report was written by the team without consultation.
verb: was written; doer: the team
The team wrote the report without consultation.

5 The trip has been organized by the social club.
verb: has been organized; doer: the social club
The social club has organized the trip.

6 Many parks in the city have been declared no-go areas by the police.
verb: have been declared; doer: the police
The police have declared many parks in the city no-go areas.

7 The man was bitten by the dog.
verb: was bitten; doer: the dog
The dog bit the man.

8 The bill was paid by her friends.
verb: was paid; doer: her friends
Her friends paid the bill.

Checklist

- Write in a way that is clear and easy to understand.
- Use correct grammar and good punctuation.
- Use everyday words if they'll do the job. For example, write *start* rather than *commence*.
- If an idea can be expressed by a noun or a verb, use the verb. For example, write *she announced* rather than *she made an announcement*.
- Use as few words as possible to get your point across clearly.
- Keep your average sentence length to 15–20 words.
- Use active verbs rather than passive verbs if you can. For example, write *the council published the report* rather than *the report was published*.

Practice exercise: Style

Let's go back to the plan that we left on page 143.

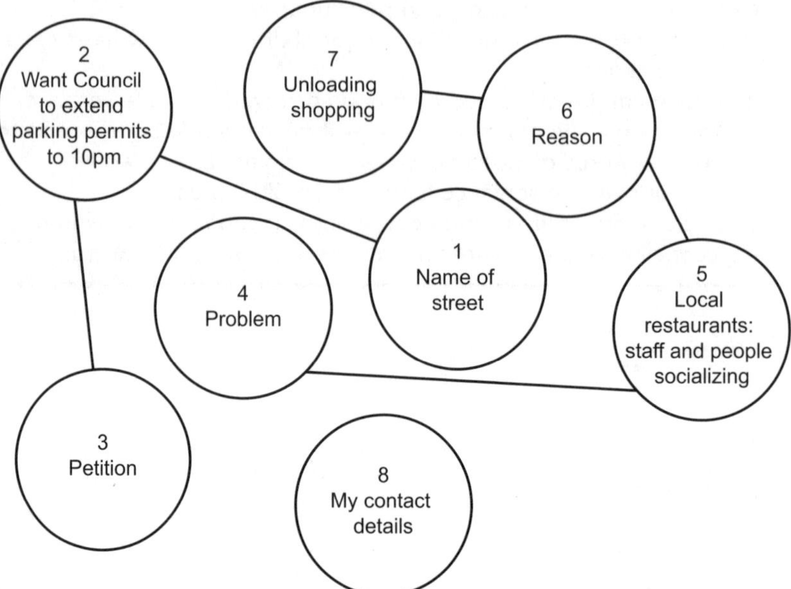

We are now in a position to start writing, putting into practice our checklist of tips about style to help us express each idea clearly.

We all express ourselves differently. Our writing style is part of our personality, and so it would be unlikely for any of us to use exactly the same combination of words and phrases to express a series of ideas. But whatever our natural writing style may be, using our checklist of tips will help us produce something readable.

Bubble 1: Heading

Think what you'd write as the heading for your letter. Here's my first idea:

Brown Street, Durham

Could we improve on this heading? We're aiming for something informative. This tells the person in the parking permit office that we're writing about this road, which is helpful. But we could use the heading to tell the reader more about the purpose of our letter:

Parking permits for Brown Street, Durham

This narrows down what the letter is about. But most letters that arrive in the parking permit section must be something to do with parking permits. Can we be even more specific about the content of the letter?

Extension to parking permits for Brown Street, Durham

This is better – can we improve still further? What are we actually doing in this letter?

Request for extension to parking permits for Brown Street, Durham

This is the best heading. The reader is fully prepared for what's to come. In fact, by using this longer heading, we've covered points 1 and 2 from the bubble diagram, so we can move straight to point 3.

Bubble 3: Petition

Think what you'd write to cover this part of the plan. Here's what I originally wrote:

> I am writing on behalf of the residents in Brown Street who have all signed a petition, which I now enclose, and want to ask you to extend the hours the parking permit is valid from 8am – 6pm to 8am – 10pm.

What do you think of that as a sentence? One obvious problem is that it contains 42 words. This is a long way over our ideal average sentence length.

We have two tactics to deal with long sentences:

- Split them into several sentences using one idea per sentence.
- Get rid of any words that don't need to be there.

A better sentence might be:

> I enclose a petition from the majority of residents of Brown Street requesting you extend our parking permit hours from 6pm at night to 10pm.

It's now 25 words. This is still a little over the ideal average sentence length, but with some shorter sentences in the rest of the letter, it should be OK. You might want to compare the two versions and see how we reduced the sentence from 42 to 25 words.

This is a good first sentence because it starts with a doer (*I*) and an active verb (*enclose*). This helps to establish a good connection between reader and writer.

But could we go further? Re-read the sentence and check for any words that do not add to the meaning.

We could reduce the sentence by two more words: *at night*. We have already written *pm*, which tells the reader that we are talking about the evening rather than the morning. So we can cut the sentence to 23 words:

> I enclose a petition from the majority of residents of Brown Street requesting you extend our parking permit hours from 6pm to 10pm.

Bubbles 4–5: Problem – local restaurants – staff and people socializing

Think what you'd write to cover this part of the plan. Here's what I originally wrote:

> The current hours for the permit are a problem due to the fact that Brown Street is in the centre of town and has many restaurants and clubs nearby so people who work in those clubs fill up our parking spaces early in the evening because they can park there after six and then later in the evening people going to the bars and clubs park in our spaces while they're having fun often until the early hours of the morning.

This covers the ideas we intended to write about from bubbles 4 and 5. But we have produced a very long sentence. This sort of sentence might work if we were speaking, but when it is written down it is tough for the reader to understand.

Again there are far too many words – 81 in fact. The problem here is that the sentence contains too many ideas. Remember that our plan had two different points that are covered by this sentence, so we can split the sentence into our two points:

- point 4: problem
- point 5: local restaurants – staff and people socializing

Let's deal with point 4 as a separate sentence:

> I'd like to explain why the current permit finishing at 6pm is a problem.

Now we can explain what the problem is (point 5). I think the explanation could be split into two sentences: the first about Brown Street's position in the centre of town near restaurants, and the second about workers and people socializing who park in the street:

> Brown Street is in the centre of town near restaurants, clubs and bars. After 6pm it provides free and convenient parking to people who work in the bars and those who socialize there.

We now have a 13-word sentence followed by a 20-word sentence. Our average sentence length is well within our limit. There is one idea per sentence, so the reader can digest the points easily.

Bubble 6–7: Reason – unloading shopping

Think what you'd write to cover this part of the plan. Here's what I originally wrote:

> The fact that cars cannot be parked by residents when they get home from work because restaurant and bar workers have parked in their spaces means residents have to pay to park further away from their homes and then struggle with their heavy shopping to their front doors.

At 48 words this is another very long sentence. It doesn't need to be so long. There are a couple of things we can do:

- Get rid of repeated ideas such as *bar and restaurant workers*, and the repeated use of *park* and *parked*.
- Split the sentence into its two main ideas: (i) there are no spaces for residents; (ii) why this makes life tough.

Have a go at re-working the sentence yourself to produce something more readable.

Bubble 6: Reason

I split the long sentence into two shorter points. Here's my second attempt to deal with point 6:

> When residents get home from work they often cannot find a parking space in Brown Street and have to pay to park further away.

This is better. Could we improve it still further? Remember that our readers want to read the message in as few words as possible.

We could simply use the verb *park* rather than the expression *find a parking space*:

> When residents get home from work they often cannot park in Brown Street and have to pay to park further away.

That's reduced the sentence length from 24 to 21 words.

Bubble 7: Unloading shopping

Here's my second attempt to deal with point 7:

> This means they have to pay to park further away from their homes and then struggle with their heavy shopping to their front doors.

That sentence is the same as the original version. It didn't work then because it was lost in a much longer sentence. Now that the idea stands on its own, it's clear.

Bubble 8: My contact details

Think what you'd write to cover this part of the plan. Here's what I originally wrote:

> Please contact me at the address on the top of this letter. I look forward to hearing from you.

Does that sound OK? There is a 12-word sentence followed by a 7-word sentence. It includes a clear and polite instruction (*Please contact me*) and a good active verb (*I look forward*).

But it seems a rather limp ending. We have followed our plan and this is where our plan finishes. Surely we've missed something out? We need a firm final sentence asking the permit office to get in touch and let us know what we need to do – if anything – to extend the permit hours:

> Please let me know what we need to do to progress this request. I will be happy to supply any further information you require. I look forward to hearing from you soon – my phone number is 03645 789456.

I've included the phone number at this point in the letter so that the reader doesn't have to scan the rest of the letter in search of it.

Paragraphs

We've now covered all of the points in our bubble diagram. I mentioned when we made our plan that we can use the links we drew on the diagram to help us decide which points could be treated together in paragraphs.

Let's now think a little more about paragraphs. The two important things we need to decide are:

- How long should they be?
- What goes into each paragraph?

I'm not going to give any specific guidelines about how long a paragraph should be. I trust you to look at your writing and decide if any paragraphs are so long that you would be put off from reading them.

We have already seen on page 130 how breaking a block of writing into paragraphs with plenty of white space can make it easier to read.

It's even OK to have a paragraph that only contains one sentence. However, a long string of paragraphs made of single sentences can be difficult to read unless the writer has grouped them under subheadings to show how they relate to each other.

When it comes to deciding what goes into a paragraph, remember that a paragraph should contain sentences about the same topic.

Look again at our original information about the parking permit problem:

> You live in a town that has had a parking permit system since 1997. The street you live in has parking down one side, but houses without driveways down both sides, so parking is always tight. Every household in the street is entitled to two parking permits. At the moment the permits cover 8am to 6pm; outside those hours anyone can park in the road. The street is near the town centre so there are restaurants and bars nearby. Much to the frustration of the majority of people in your street, if you try to park your car in the street around 6pm or later, it's virtually impossible. Early in the evening, spaces are taken up by people who work in the nearby restaurants, later in the evening it's people going out in town who park there. Someone in the street said they'd write to the Council asking for the hours of the permit to be extended until 10pm instead of 6pm. This would mean people from the street had a better chance of parking close to home. Everyone in the street thought this was a great idea and willingly signed a petition. But the letter hasn't been sent (or written) yet. You've decided to write it to try to get everything moving: you're fed up carrying your shopping to your front door from 500 yards away.

We know by looking at the paragraph that it is too long. It looks off-putting to the reader, so we need to see if we can divide it into smaller paragraphs. Look at it again, and decide where the breaks could come.

I decided that I would split this into four smaller paragraphs:

- background information: *You live ... parking is always tight.*
- the permit situation: *Every household ... park in the road.*
- the problem after 6pm: *The street ... who park there.*
- the action being taken: *Someone in the street ... 500 yards away.*

Did you agree with the way I broke up the information?

Checklist

- Break up your writing into paragraphs to make it easier to read.
- All the sentences in a paragraph should be about the same topic.

The final stage of the PROCESS method

I have nearly finished explaining the PROCESS method. So far we have talked about:

Purpose
R
O
Content
E
Structure
Style

If you use what we've looked at so far, you should be able to produce a good first version of any piece of writing:

- You will have a clear idea of your **purpose** and the people you are writing for.
- The **content** will be suitable for this purpose.
- You will have organized your points in a logical **structure**, and the document will look good.
- The **style** of language you have used will be clear, grammatically correct, well punctuated and easy to understand the first time the reader reads it through.

This all sounds good, but let's not be too quick to send your e-mail, or to put the note on your boss's desk, or to put the application in the envelope and pop it in the post.

There are two excellent reasons why you should not be too hasty:

- Even professional writers expect to read through what they've written and make a few changes and corrections.
- We still have the letters ROE to fit into our P**RO**C**E**SS method.

The letters ROE stand for **Revision Of Everything**.

This is the last stage in the writing process: to check everything to make sure that what you've written makes sense.

Checking your writing

Checking your work needs more attention than most reading. Here are some important things to think about:

- You need to make your eyes look at every word. When we read instinctively, our eyes often jump over four or five words at a time. Our brain and eyes can work cleverly together and skip over things that are wrong as long as they can understand the general sense.

- Be aware that something you wrote yourself is harder to check than something that someone else wrote. Your brain often reads what you intended to write rather than what is actually there.
- For this reason, leave a pause between finishing writing and starting to check your work.
- Some things are really important to get right, such as the name of the person you are writing to or the name of the organization you're applying to for a job. Check these especially carefully: getting them wrong could be disastrous!
- If you're using a computer, it's always worth running the spellchecker over your document. This will at least show you any words you've typed that don't exist. But remember that the spellchecker does not find everything that's wrong – it won't point out that you typed *stated* when you meant *started* or *lice* when you meant *live*. So you always need to read your document as well.
- Keep a dictionary by your side to check words if you're not sure of the correct spelling or meaning.

Here is a simple piece of writing for you to check:

Can you see what is wrong with this this headline?

How did you go about checking that headline? How long did it take you to spot the error?

Tips for checking your work:

- **Use a ruler** or piece of paper to mask the text below the line you are checking. That stops your eyes wandering further down the page without your permission.
- **Read aloud** or at least say the words to yourself as you point at each one.
- **Do it slowly.** The moment you start to hurry you'll miss something.
- **Stop** as soon as you realize you're not concentrating fully.

Now test yourself

Check the following short paragraphs and note any mistakes. Look at pages 226–7 to find out if you spotted them all.

1 They decided to leave the island and head for home a week or to early. Chris had been happy to play tennis with her friend's up until them, but she'd become keen to leave as soon as they ran out of money.

2 Some people say that texting on mobile phones will become the new way to write. Not for many years I'd say! I imagine you've heard about the 13-year-old scotish schoolgirl who shocked her teachers by writing an essay entirely in in text message shorthand. She did'nt get a very good grade. Did you know that the first text message was sent in December 992, but that it didn't really have a bid following until the early 2000s. Every hour in the Uk over two million text messages are sent and in 2003 on New year's day over 100 million we sent.

Here's the final version of the letter about parking permits we put together earlier. We've used the letter to take us through all the stages of writing. So now here it is for you to check. The time you've spent away from it will help you to look at it with fresh eyes. Look at pages 227–8 to see if you spotted all the mistakes.

Dear Sir / Madam

Request for extension to parking permits for Bown Street, Durham

I enclose a petiton from the majority of residents of Brown Street requesting you extend our parking permit hours from 6pm to 10pm.

I'd like to explain why the current permit finishing at 6pm is a problem. The residential properties in Brown Street is in the centre of town near restaurants, clubs and bars. After 6pm it provides free and convenient parking to people who work in the bars and those who socialize there.

When residents get home from work they often cannot park in in Brown Street and have to pay to park further away. This means they have to pay to park further away from their homes and then struggle with their heavy shopping to their front doors.

Please let me know what we need do to progress this request. I will be happy to supply any further information you require. I look forward to hearing from you soon – my phone number is 03645 789456.

Yours faithfully

Lynne Walker
Brown Street residents' representative

Checklist

- Check your writing carefully before you send it.
- Check your work carefully and slowly – checking is not the same as normal reading.
- Leave a pause between finishing writing and starting to check your work.

PART E

WRITING DIFFERENT TYPES OF DOCUMENT

Putting the PROCESS method into practice

You now have a method that you can apply to any writing task: the PROCESS method. This involves thinking about your **purpose**, the **content**, the right **structure** and **style**, and then making a careful **revision of everything**.

Practise this method until it becomes automatic. It will help you write:

- clearly
- to the point
- for your audience
- in as few words as possible
- in less time

We'll now look at different types of writing task and I'll give you some tips about each one. Most of all you'll get plenty of practice with the PROCESS method of writing and see examples for you to compare your writing with.

Writing a note

Some people would say that most notes are so short that there's no need to plan them. Maybe you don't need to create a bubble diagram before writing a short note, but you do need to gather your thoughts before you write. This will save you time in the long run. We usually write notes by hand. If you don't plan before you start, you might end up re-thinking half way through and crossing out chunks of text. And that never makes for an easy-to-read document.

Tips:

- Keep it brief.
- Make sure it's complete.
- Make sure it's neat enough to read.
- Read it through before you send it.

Let's look at some notes and see if they could be improved.

Note to the milkman

> *Please can I order additional items next week as I have my family staying with me for the Christmas period. In addition to my usual milk order can I have (for delivery on Monday): 12 free range eggs. 4 cartons of orange juice. A 22 lb turkey and a 'family special' box of biscuits.*
>
> *Thank you*

What do you think? Is there anything you could do to make it clearer for the milkman? Think about your purpose. The key points that your milkman needs to know are:

- what you want
- when you need it

To make this information more obvious to the milkman you could:

- write the things you want as a list with bullet points
- emphasize the day you want the things delivered

This note might be an improvement:

> *Please can I order additional items next week as I have my family staying with me for the Christmas period. In addition to my usual milk order can I have (for delivery on Monday):*
>
> - *12 free range eggs*
> - *4 cartons of orange juice*
> - *a 22lb turkey*
> - *a 'family special' box of biscuits*
>
> *Thank you*

Note to a colleague

> *Dear Julia*
> *Mr Jones phoned and left a message for you. The meeting at the Central Hotel on Thursday has been postponed. They can't do 10am now. Can you ring him to confirm that you can make it at the new time.*
> *Patricia*

How would you feel if a colleague left this note for you? Would you be able to do what she wanted?

It would be helpful to:

- know the new time for the meeting before you phone
- be given Mr Jones's phone number on the note

This note might be an improvement:

> *Dear Julia*
> *Mr Jones phoned and left a message for you. The meeting at 10am at the Central Hotel on Thursday has been postponed until 11am on Monday. Please can you ring him today on 07777 654322 to confirm that you can make this new time.*
> *Patricia*

Note to a colleague who does the next shift

> *Hello Sahia*
>
> *I've finished scanning the files from the ~~green box~~ red box up to October 2003. Can you not do the ones in the ~~same~~ red box after October 200~~32~~2, just continue from the Oct 2003 folders. Then can you continue with the blue box as much as you can do before you go home at 5pm. ~~Don't forget to make~~ Please make a copy of any docs that are stapled to the main forms. I looked at some of the folders the girl last week did and they aren't right. We need to finish all the boxes by Thursday. Do you think we will? Please leave me a note to explain how far you've got and if you have had any problems.*

There are several reasons why this is not easy to read:

- The document is a single slab of text. It could have been much better spaced, using bullet points and leaving white space around the key points.
- The key points about where to start and what to scan have crossings out. You don't necessarily have to start again if you make a mistake when writing by hand, but correction fluid or neat crossing out will help. This looks like a document that needed to be planned, but wasn't.
- It includes content that doesn't need to be there. Why worry someone about the mistakes someone else has made? The note needs to be a clear instruction about what to do rather than a grumble about what someone else got wrong.

This note might be an improvement:

Hello Sahia

I've finished scanning the files up to October 2003 from the red box.
Please:

- *scan from the Oct 2003 folders in the red box*
- *continue with the blue box as much as you can do before you go home at 5pm*
- *leave the ones in the red box after October 2002*

Remember to make a copy of any docs that are stapled to the main forms.

Do you think we will finish all the boxes by Thursday? Just leave me a note to explain how far you've got and if you have had any problems.

Brief notes

Some notes can be very brief indeed. Often we're in a real hurry and we abbreviate words or even miss some out just to make the job of writing quicker. But writing a note more quickly may make it harder for the reader to understand. And if the reader doesn't understand the message then we have wasted our time.

What do you think of these notes for the milkman?

One extra pint today and tomorrow, thanks

No milk until 28th. Thanks

Will the reader be able to understand what is needed? The second note leaves me wondering whether the writer expects milk today.

Note to a teacher explaining absence

> *Mr Peters*
> *Kelly missed school because toothache yesterday.*
> *Kelly's mum*

Would you be happy to receive this note? There are two things missing:

- a date
- at least one word

This might be an improvement:

> *10 July*
>
> *Dear Mr Peters*
>
> *Kelly missed school yesterday (9 July) because she had toothache.*
>
> *Sonja Bracken (Kelly's mum)*

A note to the doctor

> *Dear Dr Malhotra*
> *I need a certificate for work. Will you give me one. Please.*
> *Michael Stern*

What are the good points to this note? Use the PROCESS method to assess how well it works:

- **purpose**: clear even if expressed rather bluntly
- **content**: incomplete – at the very least the patient needs to supply dates
- **structure**: the key point comes first, which is good
- **style**: rather blunt – the patient seems to include 'please' as an afterthought

This might be an improvement:

> *Dear Dr Malhotra*
>
> *Request for medical certificate*
>
> *Thank you for seeing me last week when I felt so unwell. I have now been at home since 25 September (8 days), resting as you recommended and I need a certificate for my employer. Is it possible for you to provide one for me without me coming to see you again – or should I make an appointment?*
>
> *Please phone me on 01234 567892.*
>
> *Michael Stern*

Now try it yourself

Use these exercises to practise writing notes. Compare what you wrote with the suggested versions on pages 229–31.

1. Write a note to a colleague to explain where you've got to in a task and what they need to do next.

2. Ask your local vegetable delivery firm to change your weekly order. As well as your usual order you need: potatoes, cabbage (only if it's fresh), salad, home-grown tomatoes, and beans (runner beans or French). Explain that this week you'll pay by cheque so ask them to leave a bill and you'll send the cheque in. Ask the delivery man to put the stuff round the side of the house.

3. Write a note to your child's school explaining you need to take your child to a dental appointment. Explain that you couldn't get an appointment outside school hours.

4. Write to your child's school explaining your son has brought the wrong sweater home. It has no name tag in it. Ask the teacher to help find your son's sweater and return the other to its owner.

Writing a list

The important things about writing a list are:

- to make sure it's complete
- to group things together where you have to

A bubble diagram (like the one we created on page 142) helps you structure the points and check you have included everything.

Another useful technique is a 'spider diagram'. This involves making a bubble for each main area, and then turning each bubble into the body of a spider by adding a leg and label for each item you need to include under that area.

Let's see how this might look:

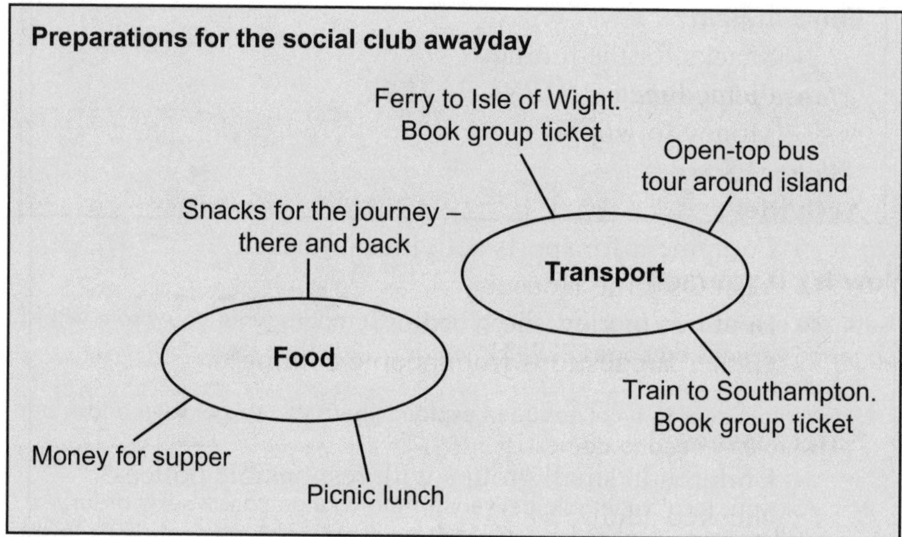

You can then turn your spider diagram into a list – if you're preparing for a meeting you might call it an 'agenda' – and use it to make sure all the jobs are taken care of:

Preparations for the social club awayday

Transport

- Train to Southampton
- Ferry to Isle of Wight
- Open-top bus tour of island

Food

- Snacks for the journey
- Picnic lunch
- Money for supper

Activities

- Equipment for sports activities on beach
- Visit Osborne House?
- Boat trip to view the Needles?
- Gather suggestions from people coming?

Safety Issues

- Children in small groups with responsible police-checked adult
- Parents encouraged to offer to help

Jobs to do

- Book transport
- Write to everyone
- Collect money
- Check cost to visit Osborne House

Now try it yourself

Use these exercises to practise writing lists. Compare what you wrote with the suggested versions on pages 232–3.

1 Write a list of things needed for a picnic for a group of families. Everyone has agreed to take what's needed, but you want to make sure you don't end up with 50 packets of crisps and nothing to drink.

2 You're off on holiday. Write a list of things you need to do before you depart.

Writing an e-mail

Even though you might think that e-mails can be treated more casually than other types of writing, the PROCESS method still applies.

Tips:

- Use a good heading to show what's in the e-mail.
- Start with a suitable greeting for your reader: *Dear Mr Banks; Hi Seeta.*
- Structure your e-mail carefully.
- Use space and subheadings to show the structure to your reader. A slab of text on the screen is probably even more off-putting than a slab of text on paper.
- Check your heading and text very carefully before you send your e-mail.

Let's look at some e-mails and see if they could be improved.

E-mail to a client

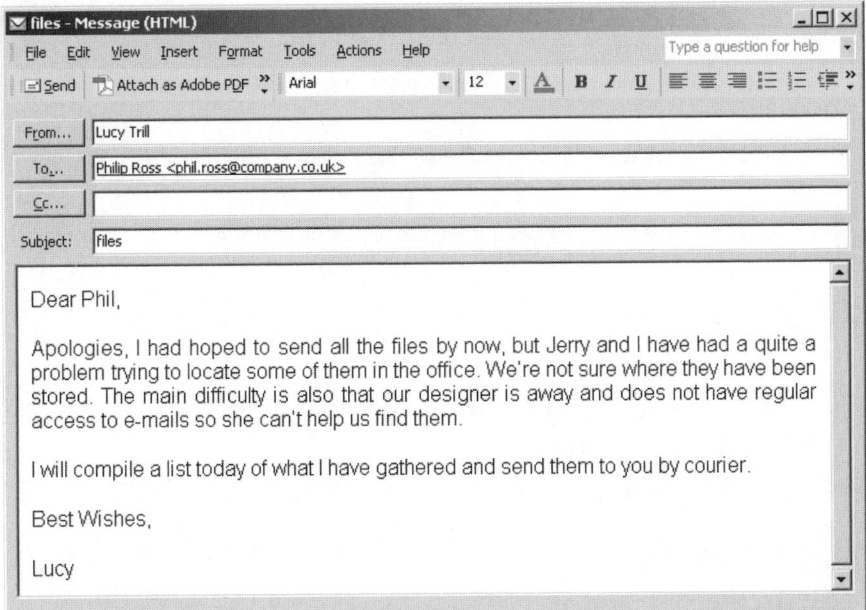

files - Message (HTML)

From... Lucy Trill

To... Philip Ross <phil.ross@company.co.uk>

Cc...

Subject: files

Dear Phil,

Apologies, I had hoped to send all the files by now, but Jerry and I have had a quite a problem trying to locate some of them in the office. We're not sure where they have been stored. The main difficulty is also that our designer is away and does not have regular access to e-mails so she can't help us find them.

I will compile a list today of what I have gathered and send them to you by courier.

Best Wishes,

Lucy

How would you like to receive this e-mail? Use the PROCESS method to assess how well it works:

- **purpose:** a well-chosen heading should help to show what the e-mail's about, but 'Files' tells us very little

- **content:** there is too much information about the inefficiencies of the organization; only relevant information is required
- **structure:** we have to wade through excuses to the last line to find what is going to happen as opposed to what is not going to happen; separating the message into paragraphs, each with its main idea, should create a good logical flow
- **style:** the point could be politely expressed in fewer words

This might be an improvement:

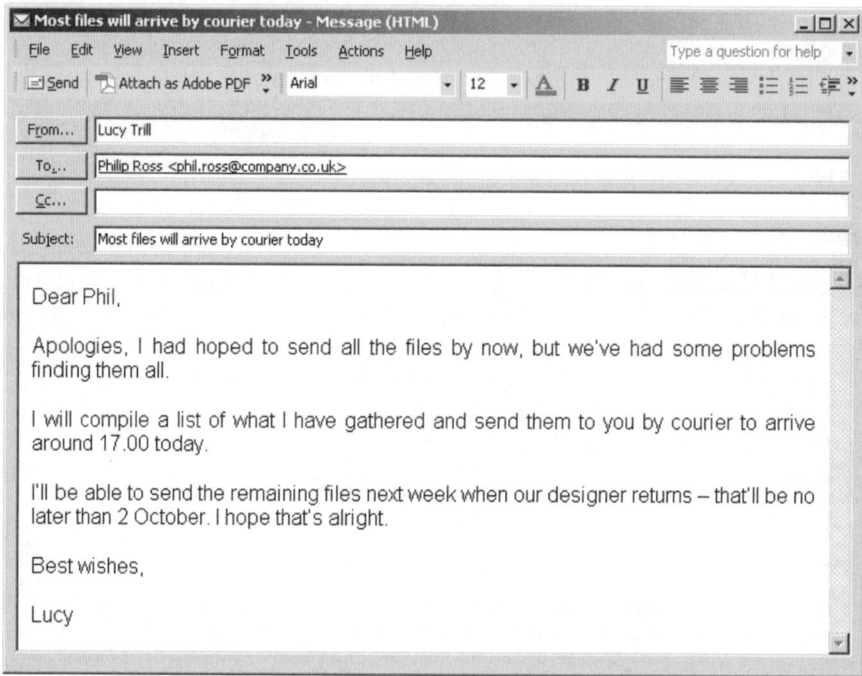

Most files will arrive by courier today - Message (HTML)

File Edit View Insert Format Tools Actions Help

From... Lucy Trill

To... Philip Ross <phil.ross@company.co.uk>

Cc...

Subject: Most files will arrive by courier today

Dear Phil,

Apologies, I had hoped to send all the files by now, but we've had some problems finding them all.

I will compile a list of what I have gathered and send them to you by courier to arrive around 17.00 today.

I'll be able to send the remaining files next week when our designer returns – that'll be no later than 2 October. I hope that's alright.

Best wishes,

Lucy

E-mail to an employee

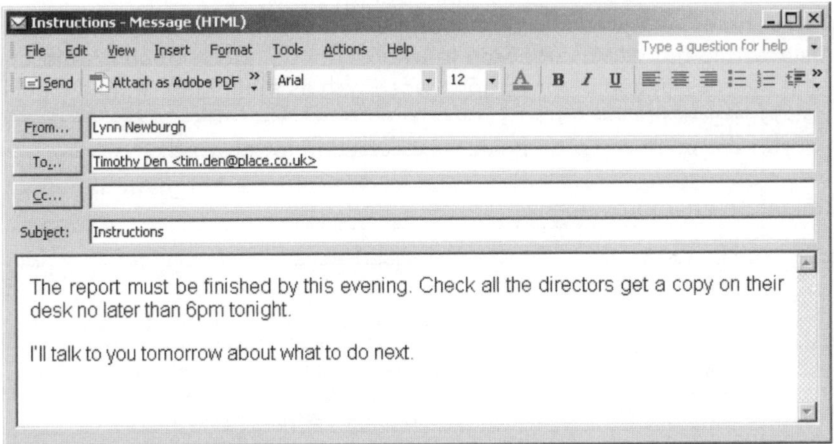

Instructions - Message (HTML)

From... Lynn Newburgh

To... Timothy Den <tim.den@place.co.uk>

Cc...

Subject: Instructions

The report must be finished by this evening. Check all the directors get a copy on their desk no later than 6pm tonight.

I'll talk to you tomorrow about what to do next.

What would you think if you received this e-mail? Use the PROCESS method to assess how well it works:

- **purpose**: the heading tells us that the purpose is to tell the reader what to do, but e-mails like this may not always achieve the writer's objective
- **content**: clear but blunt; the lack of greeting or encouragement in the e-mail may make the reader angry – it costs nothing to be courteous
- **structure**: reasonably clear
- **style**: concise, blunt and discourteous; the final sentence could be changed so that it is less like a military order and closer to a polite request

This might be an improvement:

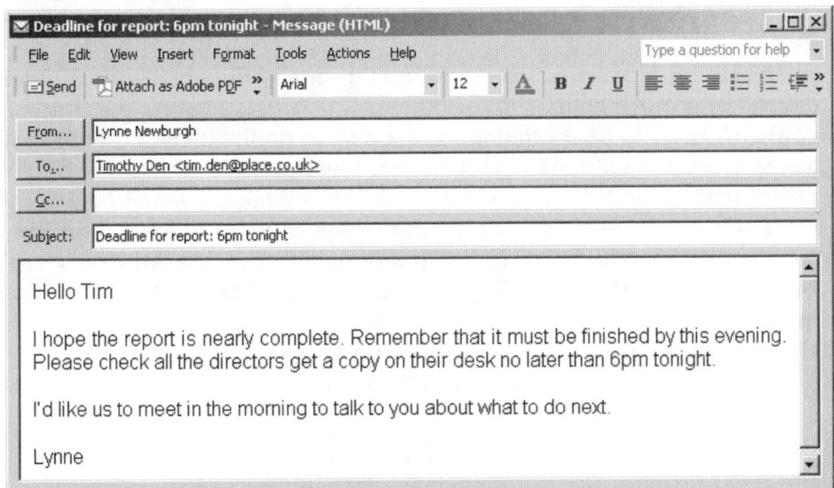

Deadline for report: 6pm tonight - Message (HTML)

From... Lynne Newburgh

To... Timothy Den <tim.den@place.co.uk>

Cc...

Subject: Deadline for report: 6pm tonight

Hello Tim

I hope the report is nearly complete. Remember that it must be finished by this evening. Please check all the directors get a copy on their desk no later than 6pm tonight.

I'd like us to meet in the morning to talk to you about what to do next.

Lynne

E-mail to a colleague explaining a business reorganization

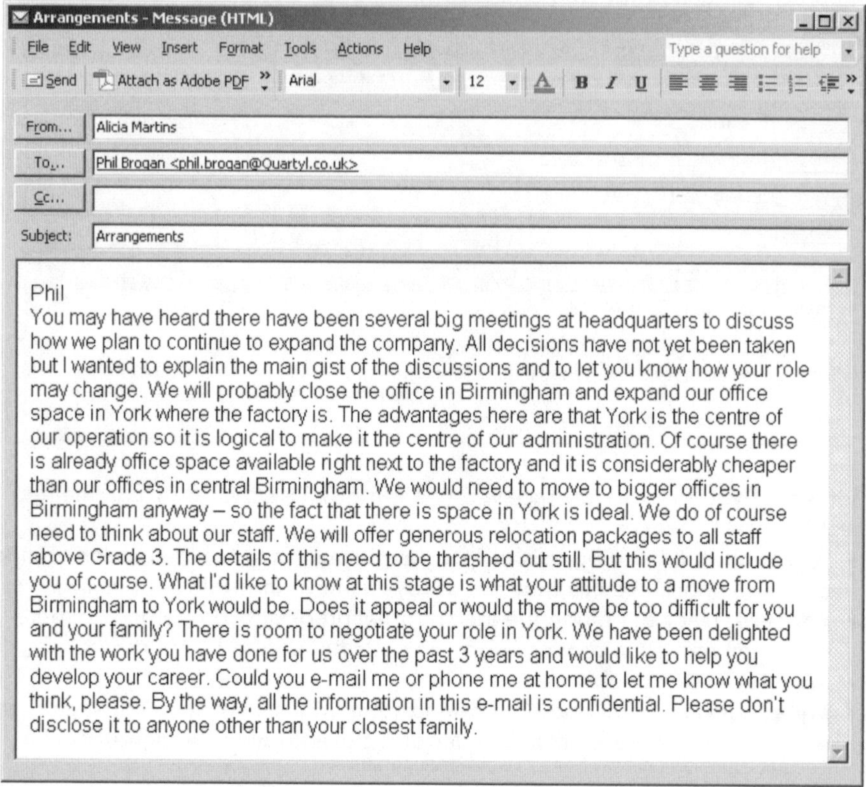

Arrangements - Message (HTML)

File Edit View Insert Format Tools Actions Help

From... Alicia Martins

To... Phil Brogan <phil.brogan@Quartyl.co.uk>

Cc...

Subject: Arrangements

Phil

You may have heard there have been several big meetings at headquarters to discuss how we plan to continue to expand the company. All decisions have not yet been taken but I wanted to explain the main gist of the discussions and to let you know how your role may change. We will probably close the office in Birmingham and expand our office space in York where the factory is. The advantages here are that York is the centre of our operation so it is logical to make it the centre of our administration. Of course there is already office space available right next to the factory and it is considerably cheaper than our offices in central Birmingham. We would need to move to bigger offices in Birmingham anyway – so the fact that there is space in York is ideal. We do of course need to think about our staff. We will offer generous relocation packages to all staff above Grade 3. The details of this need to be thrashed out still. But this would include you of course. What I'd like to know at this stage is what your attitude to a move from Birmingham to York would be. Does it appeal or would the move be too difficult for you and your family? There is room to negotiate your role in York. We have been delighted with the work you have done for us over the past 3 years and would like to help you develop your career. Could you e-mail me or phone me at home to let me know what you think, please. By the way, all the information in this e-mail is confidential. Please don't disclose it to anyone other than your closest family.

What do you think of this e-mail? Use the PROCESS method to assess how well it works:

- **purpose:** unclear unless you read right through the e-mail – the heading doesn't give much help
- **content:** likely to be shattering for the person on the receiving end, so it needs more careful handling than it has been given
- **structure:** the writer seems to be pouring out thoughts without a plan; more worryingly, the important point that the contents of the e-mail are confidential is left to the end – could the reader have unintentionally broken the confidentiality by telling someone in the office what's afoot before he gets to the last line?
- **style:** some phrases are repeated, suggesting that the e-mail wasn't planned beforehand or read through afterwards

Let's address these criticisms and improve the e-mail. Have a go yourself and then compare your version with the one below:

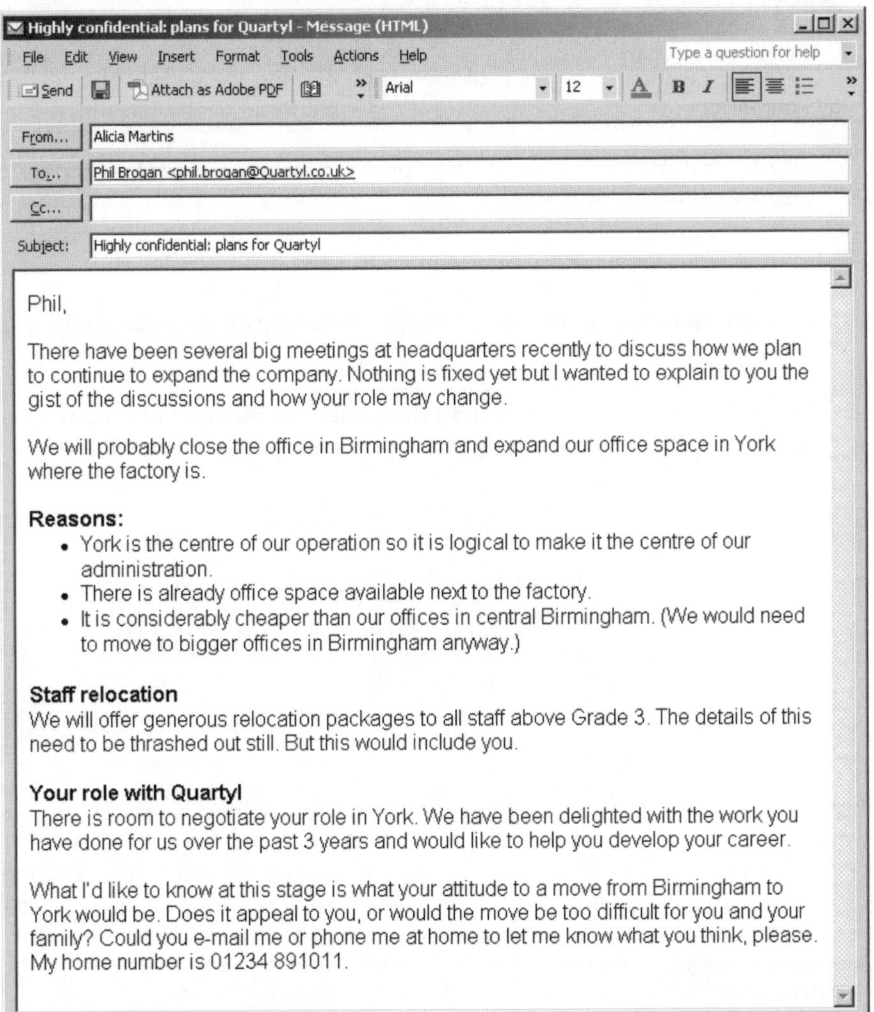

Highly confidential: plans for Quartyl - Message (HTML)

From... Alicia Martins

To... Phil Brogan <phil.brogan@Quartyl.co.uk>

Cc...

Subject: Highly confidential: plans for Quartyl

Phil,

There have been several big meetings at headquarters recently to discuss how we plan to continue to expand the company. Nothing is fixed yet but I wanted to explain to you the gist of the discussions and how your role may change.

We will probably close the office in Birmingham and expand our office space in York where the factory is.

Reasons:

- York is the centre of our operation so it is logical to make it the centre of our administration.
- There is already office space available next to the factory.
- It is considerably cheaper than our offices in central Birmingham. (We would need to move to bigger offices in Birmingham anyway.)

Staff relocation

We will offer generous relocation packages to all staff above Grade 3. The details of this need to be thrashed out still. But this would include you.

Your role with Quartyl

There is room to negotiate your role in York. We have been delighted with the work you have done for us over the past 3 years and would like to help you develop your career.

What I'd like to know at this stage is what your attitude to a move from Birmingham to York would be. Does it appeal to you, or would the move be too difficult for you and your family? Could you e-mail me or phone me at home to let me know what you think, please. My home number is 01234 891011.

Now try it yourself

Use these exercises to practise writing e-mails. Compare what you wrote with the suggested versions on pages 234–8.

1 Write an e-mail to a group of friends confirming the details of a meeting.

2 Write an e-mail to the doctor's surgery requesting a repeat prescription for some medicine.

3 E-mail your local library asking them to reserve a book for you.

4 E-mail your boss asking if it's OK for you to book two weeks' holiday in July.

5 E-mail the committee explaining what needs to be done to prepare the village hall for a fund-raising event and asking for volunteers.

Filling in a form

There are various different types of form you might have to fill in:

- passport application
- credit card application
- benefit form
- job application form
- tax form

Filling in forms can be a tiresome and difficult task. Forms can take ages to fill in, and the questions may seem strange – it can be difficult to know what they want. But forms can be very important: sometimes a lot depends on filling in a form correctly.

So it's worth taking time to think about what you need to do.

You may think some of my suggestions will take you a long time to go through.

Yes, you're right, some really will take you a long time to do. But it's worth it. If you get the form wrong in some way, you may:

- delay your application by days or weeks because they return it to you to correct
- not get the thing you're applying for at all

I'm sure you can think of other problems!

Before you write anything ...

Don't rush in and start trying to fill in a form straight away. Go through these steps:

- Read the form through to check what's expected. Do you need to get other information or documents before you can answer the questions? It's a good idea to gather these before you start.
- Read the notes if there are any – the most user-friendly forms will display the notes somewhere you can find them easily. Continue to look at them while you're filling in the form.
- If it's a form it would be difficult to get another copy of, photocopy it before you start to fill it in. (If it's got colour on it, use a colour photocopier.) This means you can either start again on the photocopy if you make a big mistake, or you can use the photocopy for a first draft. You can then check your answers and when you're sure they're what you want, write them out again onto the real form.

When you write

Proceed slowly and carefully. On some forms you are not allowed to cross out anything. So if you make a mistake you must start again. Here are some tips:

- Use the right colour pen. Many forms ask you to use black ink because they're going to be photocopied. (A friend recently told me she'd started to complete a passport form in blue ink – only the first two words – before she realized it should be black. She went over the blue ink with a black pen. They sent the form back to her to re-do. That delayed the passport by at least a week!)
- Use the same pen throughout, if you can. Different pens can make the form look untidy.
- Do what the notes say! If it says on a form *Keep your signature inside the box*, then do just that. If you don't, you could increase the time it takes to process the form – and you may have to fill in the whole form again from scratch.
- Use BLOCK CAPITALS if that's what they ask you to do.
- If you're writing letters in individual boxes, make sure your letters fit into the boxes properly. The letters A and D can look similar, as can J and T, and 1 and 7, so take care to write these clearly.
- Write neatly. At the very least, make sure the person who will deal with the form can read your writing.
- Make sure that what you write is accurate. Check things like dates and addresses.
- Check as far as you can that you're giving the information they want. Sometimes forms are not well written or designed and that's why we find them such hard going. If you're not sure, get help. Many forms have a helpline number on them or details of a website to guide you.

After you have completed the form

Don't be in a hurry to send the form off as soon you finish it. Read it through and check that you've filled **everything** in:

- Make sure you haven't missed out any questions on the back of the form.
- Some forms have two columns – it's easy to forget to fill in the answers on the right-hand column.
- Make sure you've included all the things you need to send with the form.
- Ask a friend to read it through to check that everything makes sense – another pair of eyes can make a big difference.

Before you put the form in the post, photocopy it, especially if it's a job application. They'll have your application in front of them at the interview. Don't put yourself at a disadvantage by not being able to check what you wrote.

Writing instructions

The important thing about giving someone written instructions is that they should be able to follow them without asking you what you mean. Remember that you may not be around to explain yourself when they try to carry them out.

I'm sure you know how frustrating and annoying it is to struggle to make sense of badly written instructions. You don't want to put other people through the same ordeal.

Tips:

- Get the sequence right.
- Use numbers or words like *first*, *then* and *next* to show the sequence.
- Test the instructions – preferably with someone who knows nothing about the subject – to be sure they work.
- Use verbs at the beginning of each instruction – just as I have in this list.
- Use subheadings to group the instructions to help the reader see where they're going in the process.
- Don't miss out the little words *and*, *the* and *a*. We need them!

Look at the instructions for someone who wants to borrow a library book on page 186. Would you be able to carry them out?

Instructions for someone who wants to borrow a library book

First join the library

1. Take two proofs of address to your local library – the one you want to join. This could be a letter sent through the post with your name and address on it, or a bill from the gas board, electricity board or from your local council.
2. Tell the person on the information desk you want to join the library.
3. They will take you through the forms, ask you to sign and most will be able to give you your borrowing card immediately.

Now you're ready to borrow a book

4. Choose the book you would like to borrow. Make sure it doesn't have 'Reference Only' printed on the cover – that would mean you can't take it home.
5. Hand the book with your library card to the librarian.
6. The librarian will stamp it with the return date – usually three weeks from the day you borrow the book – and return it to you with your card.

Remember:

- **You can borrow up to 12 books – 6 fiction and 6 non-fiction.**
- **You can renew a book by phone or e-mail, or by going into the library.**
- **You will have to pay a fine if you don't get the book back before or on the right day.**

What do you think of these instructions? Use the PROCESS method to assess how well they work:

- **purpose**: clear
- **content**: all the important information is there
- **structure**: the information is presented in the right order, with first things first; the use of numbers and subheadings makes the procedure easy to follow
- **style**: there are no unnecessarily difficult words; the sentences are a manageable length; and there are lots of active verbs

So these instructions should be easy to follow.

Now try it yourself

Use these exercises to practise writing instructions. Compare what you wrote with the suggested versions on pages 239–41.

1. Write some short instructions on how to make a cup of tea.
2. Write a set of road safety instructions for children at a primary school.
3. Write a set of instructions for an adult who has agreed to supervise the bouncy castle at the village fete.

Writing a letter

As with other types of writing, you can use the PROCESS method to plan, write and revise a letter. This is especially the case with a formal letter, but even for a letter to a close friend, it helps to think about why you are writing and what you want to achieve.

There are certain features that all letters should have:

- your address on the top right-hand side of the letter
- the date
- a greeting
- a sign-off phrase

For a formal letter, you should include:

- the address of the person you are writing to, on the left-hand side at the top of the letter
- a heading saying what the letter is about

Tips:

- Choose an informative heading. A well-chosen heading can draw the reader into your letter. No heading or a rather general one may mean the reader doesn't see straight away why they need to read it, so they might put the letter down and get on with the next task on their pile.
- Start with a verb. *Thank you for...* or *I refer to...* will help you control the length of your first sentence.
- Make the layout look good. Make sure there is plenty of white space and that paragraphs are kept to a reasonable length. Use subheadings as well as the main heading if necessary.
- Get the greeting and sign-off right. If you start *Dear Sir / Madam*, end with *Yours faithfully*; if you start *Dear Mr...*, *Dear Mrs ...*or *Dear Miss...*, end with *Yours sincerely*. (Note that you shouldn't use a capital letter for *faithfully* or *sincerely*.)
- Make sure the name and address of the recipient are correct. Nobody likes their name to be spelt incorrectly; if you make a mistake with the address, the letter may never reach its destination.

Here is an example of how these features might appear:

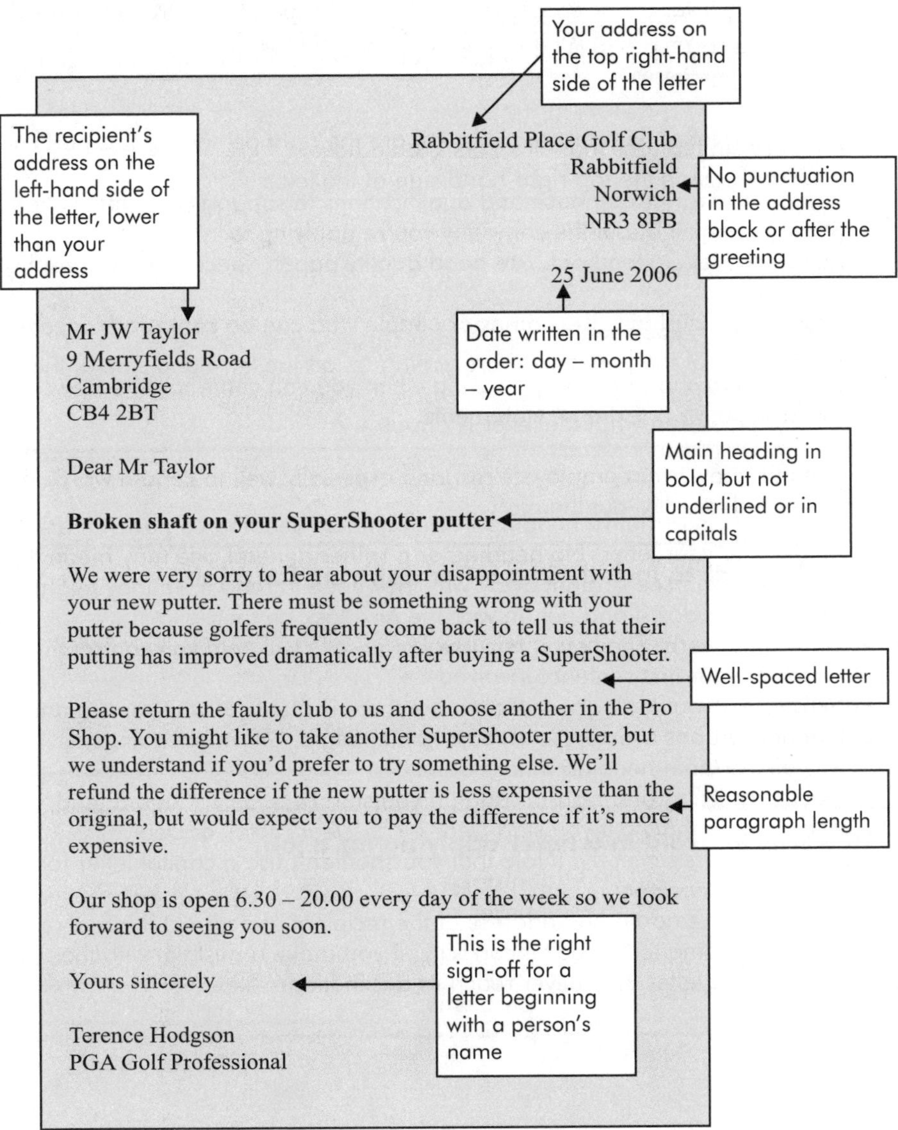

Rabbitfield Place Golf Club
Rabbitfield
Norwich
NR3 8PB

25 June 2006

Mr JW Taylor
9 Merryfields Road
Cambridge
CB4 2BT

Dear Mr Taylor

Broken shaft on your SuperShooter putter

We were very sorry to hear about your disappointment with your new putter. There must be something wrong with your putter because golfers frequently come back to tell us that their putting has improved dramatically after buying a SuperShooter.

Please return the faulty club to us and choose another in the Pro Shop. You might like to take another SuperShooter putter, but we understand if you'd prefer to try something else. We'll refund the difference if the new putter is less expensive than the original, but would expect you to pay the difference if it's more expensive.

Our shop is open 6.30 – 20.00 every day of the week so we look forward to seeing you soon.

Yours sincerely

Terence Hodgson
PGA Golf Professional

The basic layout of this letter is a good model to follow. In the following pages we'll look at some important types of letter that you might have to write.

A covering letter to apply for a job

This is obviously a very important letter and it's worth spending extra time to make sure that you get everything right and create a good impression.

Tips:

- Make your letter demonstrate why you are the right person for this particular job.
- Pick out relevant experience and qualifications to support your application.
- Show you know about the company you're applying to.
- Make your letter stand out: use good quality paper; space the paragraphs out well.
- Attach a CV and give the names of people who can be contacted for references.
- Finish with a short paragraph saying when you can come for interview.
- Avoid negative or extreme statements.

Research has shown that employers respond especially well to certain words, but that other words tend to put them off.

Top 10 words to include in a letter applying for a job

achievement
active
developed
evidence
experience
impact
individual
involved
planning
transferable skills

10 words to avoid in a letter applying for a job

always
awful
bad
fault
hate
mistake
never
nothing
panic
problems

Take a look at these two applications for the same job. Who would you call for interview?

Holly Cottage
Fullers Lane
Oldbury

Ms L Jacobs
Oldbury Insurance
13 Old Street
Oldbury

18 April 2006

Dear Ms Jacobs

Further to your advertisement in the Salisbury Recorder dated 17 April, I am applying for the position of Chief Receptionist at your Head Office in Old Street. I enclose a copy of my CV and a supporting statement as requested.

I have five years' experience of work as a receptionist for my current employer and am used to dealing with a broad range of customers and clients. In my latest job appraisal, my quick thinking and pleasant manner were highly commended by my line manager.

I feel I am now ready to move to a position which will give me more responsibility and offer a greater challenge.

I hope you consider my application to be suitable.

Yours sincerely

Brenda Reilly (Ms)

Ms L Jacobs
Oldbury Insurance
13 Old Street
Oldbury

Dear Madam,

I would like to apply for the job of receptionist with your company. I have plenty of experience. I have worked for three years as the receptionist at the Blue Goose Hotel and before that for two years at the Castle Inn. I enjoy my job but I don't get on with the new manager who took over earlier this year so I want to find a new position.

I am also qualified for the job. I studied for a GNVQ in hotel administration at Oldbury College and graduated in 2000.

As you can see, I am an ideal candidate for your job. I hope you will give me an interview.

Jane Jackson

Let's compare the two letters:

	Brenda Reilly	**Jane Jackson**
address	both addresses included and positioned correctly	home address not included on letter
date	date in correct position	no date
greeting	*Dear Ms Jacobs* is the correct use of title and surname – the initial is not part of the title	*Dear Madam* is not a good start – always use the person's name if you have it
main part of the letter	• clear opening sentence – although it could be divided into two sentences and begin with a verb: *I would like to apply…* • highlights experience and skills that will be useful for the job: *dealing with a broad range of customers and clients; my quick thinking and pleasant manner were highly commended by my line manager* • includes a positive reason for wanting to move on	• clear opening sentence – but the writer should refer to the advertisement • mentions a paper qualification but doesn't highlight key skills that might be relevant • the applicant *hopes* for an interview but has told us nothing of her skills other than the unsupported and unconvincing *I am an ideal candidate* • reference to *I don't get on with the new manager* may set alarm bells ringing
CV	encloses a CV	no mention of a CV
sign-off	*Yours sincerely* is the correct sign-off after you address someone by their name	no sign-off included
title of applicant	title *(Ms)* appears after the typewritten name, so a reply can be addressed correctly	no mention of applicant's title, so replier will have to guess how to address her

There's not much doubt as to which of the two is more likely to get an interview.

Writing a letter of complaint

The purpose of writing this sort of letter is usually to get an apology, a refund or a replacement, so you should keep this in mind when you think about your content, structure and style.

Tips:

- The heading should include the problem.
- Detail what has happened and what action you want the recipient to take in the first paragraph.
- Do not become angry or rude in the letter – it rarely helps you to get a better result.
- Have all the facts at your fingertips: dates, products, references, receipts, guarantees, what happened.
- Keep copies of all correspondence and enclosures that you send.

Imagine you are the manager of a sporting goods store. You receive these two letters of complaint. You need to deal with both letters, but which will you take more seriously, and why?

P March
Oldbury

The Manager
Sportstime
7 The High Street

Dear Manager,

I bought a pair of trainers at your shop last week but when I wore them they split. I took them back to the shop and the assistant was really rude and told me that it was my fault. I don't think that it is my fault and I want a refund because they must have been faulty when I was sold them.

Please will you do something about this matter.

Yours, etc.

P March (Miss)

6 The Crescent,
Oldbury
OD1 9JK

The Manager
Sportstime
7 The High Street
Oldbury
OD4 4SP

17 March 2006

Dear Sir

Faulty trainers
I bought a pair of trainers at your shop, Sportstime, at 7 The High Street, on 13 March. I enclose a copy of the receipt.

Unfortunately, the trainers split when I wore them the following day.

I visited your shop to return the shoes on 15 March but was told that the shop's policy is not to give refunds. I asked to speak to you personally but was told that you were not available.

Under my statutory rights, I am entitled to a full refund as the trainers were clearly unfit for sale. I would appreciate it if you can arrange a refund, otherwise I shall be making an official complaint.

I look forward to receiving your reply as soon as possible.

Yours faithfully

C Robinson (Mrs)

Let's compare the two letters:

	Miss March	**Mrs Robinson**
address	sender's address is incomplete, so there is no way of replying	correctly positioned and complete
date	no date	date in correct position
greeting	*Dear Manager* is not a good start	*Dear Sir* is the correct title if you know the person's gender but not his name
main part of the letter	• no heading • no mention of receipts or legal rights • *Please will you do something about this matter* is rather vague: does this refer to the rude assistant or arranging a refund?	• use of heading makes it clear what the letter is about • all important details of the purchase are explained • the writer makes it clear she knows her legal entitlements • clear expression of what the writer wants to be done
sign-off	*Yours, etc* is not a suitable sign-off for a formal letter like this one	*Yours faithfully* is the correct sign-off after you address someone as *Dear Sir*

Miss March may have a good case for a refund, but she is unlikely to receive one unless she takes care to give the information that is needed.

Now try it yourself

Use these exercises to practise writing letters. Compare what you wrote with the suggested versions on pages 242–4.

1. Write to the head teacher at your son's primary school asking for permission for him to miss the last four days of term because you want to take him on holiday. Provide a reasonable excuse.

2. Plan and write a letter on behalf of your local social club to try to make up the differences between your group and another youth group on the other side of the city. There has been rivalry between the two groups, but a united front could gain much for both groups.

3. Plan and write a letter of complaint to the council about the poor facilities for young people in your area. There is plenty for the age group 11–14, but young people older than that don't seem to have anywhere to go.

ANSWERS TO LANGUAGE QUIZ AND EXERCISES

Answers to Language Quiz

1 c. ran
2 a. decided
3 c. loves
4 a. opted
5 c. arrived

6 a. road
7 c. garden
8 b. light
9 a. help
10 a. pen

11 c. green
12 c. new
13 c. expensive
14 b. heavy
15 a. remote

16 c. enthusiastically
17 a. slowly
18 c. methodically
19 b. willingly
20 b. generously

21 a. Alex
22 b. managers
23 b. school
24 b. he
25 c. cats

26 c. hitchhiker
27 a. apple
28 a. boat
29 a. policy
30 a. sandwich

31 **She** wanted to invite her friends to the house.
32 The teacher asked **me** to pass the book to my friend.
33 Where did **you** get such thick paper?
34 **They** asked the group to meet at the pub.
35 Take these extra tickets for **them**.

36 incorrect
37 correct
38 incorrect
39 incorrect
40 incorrect
41 incorrect
42 incorrect
43 incorrect
44 incorrect

45 incorrect
46 correct
47 incorrect
48 correct
49 incorrect

50 incorrect
51 correct
52 incorrect
53 incorrect
54 incorrect

55 complete
56 incomplete
57 incomplete
58 incomplete
59 complete

60 Alex and Nick wandered home from the park**. T**hey had had a great afternoon playing with their friends**. T**hey intended to have a quick supper and finish their homework**. U**nfortunately when they got home around 6pm supper wasn't ready.

61 Where did you spend the last week in January**?**
62 no question mark is needed

63 That's an absolutely amazing dog**!** I've never seen one so huge**!**

64 He bought butter**,** margarine**,** sugar**,** salt and flour.
65 Liz**,** my best friend from school**,** keeps in touch regularly.
66 If you want to help the students**,** learn the subject yourself first.

67 He told us what we'd learn: how to drill the right size holes in a wall, how to use Rawlplugs, and how to put up a shelf.
68 Bring everything you'll need for a week in freezing conditions: warm underwear, thick sweaters and trousers, decent walking boots, and a thick waterproof coat with a hood.

69 I'm not sure if he's coming to the meal this evening or even if you're coming.
70 The teachers' reports were stacked high in the classrooms.
71 The manager's decision has made everyone unhappy.
72 The dog's dinner's in its bowl.
73 It's never too late to change.
74 That table's got to go – it's almost falling apart it's so unsafe.

75 b. know
76 c. have
77 a. quite
78 c. their
79 b. wear
80 a. whose
81 b. brought
82 b. practise
83 a. licence
84 b. accept
85 b. alternative
86 b. lend
87 a. effect
88 b. lain
89 c. breathe
90 b. stationary

Answers to exercises in Part A

Exercises on page 17

1 John **ordered** two beers and a glass of red wine.

2 The kids **ran** down the hill at top speed.

3 Alex **was running** into school when the bell **rang**.

4 Peter **said** he **had put** the shopping in the fridge.

5 The meal **should have been** ready hours ago.

6 The tickets **were sold** as soon as they **appeared**.

7 He **didn't watch** the TV programme.

8 They **have finished** the book already.

9 They **were helping** their friends.

10 When **are** they **leaving**?

11 He **might have gone** to the coast.

12 You **must finish** the curtains by lunchtime.

13 Ros **has** just **phoned** me about her daughter's exam results.

14 The windows **were cleaned** last Thursday.

15 The director **couldn't understand** the problem.

16 He **applied** for the job and **got** it.

Exercises on page 21

1 The dog **chased** the cats.

2 The sausages **are being cooked**.

3 Mira and her friend **will arrive** before 8pm.

4 John **must announce** the team soon.

5 We'**ll meet up** next week.

6 They **wanted to celebrate** the occasion.

7 **Eat** plenty of fresh fruit.

8 **Cut down** on the doughnuts!

9 Any decision **should be checked** carefully.

10 They **need to learn** their lines by Saturday.

11 She **couldn't have predicted** their reaction.

12 He **seemed** genuinely surprised about the robbery.

13 She **felt** sorry for him.

14 They **must have taken** their parents' car.

Exercises on page 24

1 **Lisa** wanted to start **school** early.

2 The **oranges** were in the **bowl**.

3 The **holidays** were over far too quickly.

4 The **manager** arranged the **meeting** for **9 June**.

5 They finished the **job** in the **time** agreed.

6 The **marathon** raised **thousands of pounds** for **charity**.

7 His **confidence** was shaken by the **appraisal**.

8 The **development** of the residential **area** has created **problems** for the **town**.

9 **Philip** treated his **employees** to a **meal** every **January**.

10 The **Eden Project** makes a memorable **day** out.

11 He hoped he'd win the **race**.

12 The **teachers** were sure she would pass her **exams**.

13 Why hasn't he finished his **project** yet?

14 After the **nightmare** she didn't want to go out.

15 **Harriet** wanted to go to **university**.

Exercises on page 27

1 The **rescue** (noun) **took** (verb) five **hours** (noun).

2 The **fireman** (noun) **rescued** (verb) the cat (noun) in under ten **minutes** (noun).

3 The **saw** (noun) **had been tested** (verb) and **was** (verb) extremely sharp.

4 **Lisa** (noun) **saw** (verb) all the **doughnuts** (noun) **disappear** (verb).

5 The **PIN number** (noun) **was** (verb) on a **slip** (noun) of **paper** (noun).

6 Don't **slip** (verb) on that **patch** (noun) of **ice** (noun) over there.

7 I **patched up** (verb) those old **trousers** (noun).

8 My **fingers** (noun) **are** (verb) too long for these **gloves** (noun).

9 She **fingered** (verb) the **material** (noun).

10 The **drink** (noun) **was made** (verb) of **brandy** (noun), **crème de cacao** (noun) and **cream** (noun).

11 What **would** (verb) you **like** (verb) **to drink** (verb)?

12 It **took** (verb) him seven **hours** (noun) **to swim** (verb) the **channel** (noun).

13 The **report** (noun) **announced** (verb) **James** (noun) **should channel** (verb) his **energies** (noun) into his **art** (noun).

14 The **damage** (noun) **will cost** (verb) **£500** (noun) **to repair** (verb).

15 Who **damaged** (verb) the **chair** (noun)?

Exercises on page 30

1 They asked for the most **expensive main** course.

2 The **successful** shop closed and moved to the **new** shopping centre.

3 Eat plenty of **green** vegetables.

4 She was invited to attend the **jazz** concert.

5 The **secondary** school announced its **new** policy on absenteeism.

6 The **delayed** start of the film meant **many** people had to leave early.

7 She chose a **cotton** blouse and a **green silk** skirt.

8 The **recent** announcement has caused uncertainty.

9 An **estate** car drew up outside the **semi-detached** house.

10 **Air** travel creates **high** levels of pollution.

Exercises on page 33

1 They **usually** get up around 7 o'clock.

2 Emily slept **soundly**.

3 She couldn't run **quickly** because her back was bad.

4 The policemen checked the evidence **thoroughly**.

5 The man played **well** and won **convincingly**.

6 The teachers nodded **encouragingly at the end of the performance**.

7 The course ended **disastrously** – no one passed the exam!

8 Why doesn't he try **hard**?

9 His book was **widely** read.

10 Sarah spoke to me **boldly** about her plans.

11 They packed their bags **at top speed**.

12 Nick played **endlessly** on the computer.

13 Alex worked on his project **in his bedroom with enthusiasm**.

14 They voted for Jones **unanimously**.

15 He criticized their work **mercilessly**.

Exercises on page 35 (1)

1 John refused to eat the **dried-up** (adjective) sandwiches.

2 The **new** (adjective) keeper performed **magnificently** (adverb).

3 The river flowed **rapidly** (adverb) though the **spectacular** (adjective) gorges.

4 The chef **instantly** (adverb) produced a **delicious** (adjective) meal for the **grateful** (adjective) travellers.

5 The tomatoes ripened **gradually** (adverb) in the **wet** (adjective) summer.

6 No amount of practice will help him play that violin **well** (adverb).

7 The beach filled up **rapidly** (adverb) with **excited** (adjective) children and their families.

8 Why don't we use **renewable** (adjective) energy sources **whenever possible** (adverb)?

Exercises on page 35 (2)

1 incorrect: He walked home **quickly**.

2 incorrect: They ran too **slowly** to catch the crowded bus.

3 incorrect: Why did he do the job so **badly**?

4 correct

5 correct

6 incorrect: They wrote the letter **neatly**.

Exercises on page 38

1 **The book** (subject) described **her journey to China** (object).

2 **Flowers** (subject) brighten up **a room** (object).

3 **The teacher** (subject) announced **the plan** (object) for the term.

4 **Chocolate cake** (subject) helps **concentration** (object).

5 **He** (subject) took **the wrong road** (object) and arrived late.

6 **I** (subject) can't help **you** (object).

7 **Solar panels** (subject) reduce **electricity consumption** (object).

8 **Weeds** (subject) grow quickly in warm weather. (there is no object)

Exercises on page 47

1 incorrect: I **want** a new toy.

2 correct

3 correct

4 incorrect: John **decides** how to run the company.

5 incorrect: He **doesn't** want to employ unqualified staff.

6 correct

7 incorrect: **Does** he have to take on qualified staff?

8 correct

9 incorrect: Ann and Mike **have** taken the decision to close the factory.

10 incorrect: The laws **are** there to protect us all.

11 incorrect: He **doesn't** have any ink left.

12 incorrect: Sally and Joe **haven't** bought the shopping.

13 incorrect: We **weren't** late for the meeting.

14 correct

15 incorrect: The children **haven't** done their homework.

16 incorrect: The sandwiches **taste** horrible.

17 incorrect: Chocolates **are** bad for your teeth.

18 correct

19 incorrect: I **was** shocked at the news.

20 incorrect: Why **aren't** they here?

Exercises on page 50

1 correct

2 incorrect: He **did** it yesterday.

3 incorrect: What has he **drunk**?

4 incorrect: They have **written** about everything they **did**.

5 incorrect: My ankle's **swollen** up horribly after the fall.

6 incorrect: They **ate** before they left.

7 incorrect: Has he **eaten** yet?

8 incorrect: He has **lain** down.

9 incorrect: She **lay** down on the sofa.

10 incorrect: I **drank** too many glasses of water.

11 incorrect: Why has he **gone** there?

12 correct

13 incorrect: They **swam** out beyond the coral reef.

14 incorrect: Has he **mown** the garden yet?

15 correct

Exercises on page 60

1 incorrect: The cat wanted to come in, so **it** banged **its** nose on the window.

2 incorrect: They told Jack and **me** to send our applications in immediately.

3 correct

4 correct

5 incorrect: The police told my manager and **me** they had already looked into the problem.

6 incorrect: The government has asked us all to look at **its** policies on health and education.

7 incorrect: The parrot was rather talkative so I gave it a sunflower seed. I can't repeat what **it** said in reply!

8 incorrect: Jane and **I** would like to come to the party on Friday.

Exercises on page 64

(There may be several different ways of correcting the incomplete sentences.)

1 correct

2 incorrect: Helen **was spending** a year in Canada.

3 incorrect: Charles flew to South America with **his family**.

4 incorrect: Cathy **is preparing** for her next trip to France.

5 incorrect: **The** documents were being prepared.

6 incorrect: With reference to your recent letter**, I am happy to enclose a cheque for £100**.

7 incorrect: **I decided** to borrow the book instead.

8 incorrect: The managers **had** a great reputation for getting things sorted.

9 incorrect: The few remaining members of the football team **met in the clubhouse**.

10 incorrect: Decisions were being **taken** slowly.

Answers to exercises in Part B

Exercises on page 81

1 They wanted to have a range of sandwiches available: cheese and pickle**,** beef and gherkin**,** tuna and mayonnaise**,** and brie and grapes.

2 Alice prepared all the equipment they needed for the trip**,** and Felix and Nigel got the food ready.

3 If you can explain to me how you happen to have a crocodile skin handbag in your suitcase**,** I will consider what action we take next.

4 Because train journeys in France are so smooth and reasonably priced**,** it's worth considering abandoning your car for the summer.

5 Following the recent downpours and flooding**,** the council has decided to invest more money in flood protection barriers.

6 He had brought sandwiches**,** pies**,** scotch eggs**,** dips**,** ice creams**,** cakes**,** sweets and fruit.

Exercises on page 83

1 He asked the first students in the register to help**:** Andrew, Jane, Guy, Tim and Cathy.

2 They couldn't believe all the things they needed to buy for the first-aid kit**:** bandages, plasters, antiseptic spray, antiseptic cream, triangular bandages, pain-killing tablets ... to name but a few items.

3 The leaflet told us what to do in an emergency power cut**:** make our way to the exit calmly and hold the hand of the person in front of and behind us.

4 They showed us how much they enjoyed the dinner we had prepared**:** they ate every morsel.

5 She loved every aspect of the garden**:** sitting in it, weeding it, picking salad leaves and simply admiring it.

6 They presented us with quite a choice of holiday destinations**:** Cuba, The Seychelles, Egypt or Venezuela.

7 He worked incredibly hard throughout his stay**:** he did the garden, renewed the fencing and painted the window frames.

8 The invitation promised a fantastic evening**:** delicious food, plenty of fine wine, a midnight swim and a jazz band.

9 She made it clear she didn't intend to stay**:** she packed her suitcase and ordered a taxi for the airport.

10 Go and gather together everything you need for the trip**:** wet gear, shorts, swimming things, sun tan cream, walking shoes, trainers and sandals.

Exercises on page 89

1 The day**'**s events were recorded on camera.

2 The headteacher**'**s solution was to take on more staff.

3 The cat**'**s not well so I must take her to see the vet.

4 This company**'**s key assets were its staff and expertise.

5 These companies**'** key assets are their premises and stock.

6 The companies have joined forces.

7 The managers agreed to implement the new strategy.

8 Who**'**s going to tell her why you**'**re late?

9 The doctors don**'**t want to increase their patients**'** waiting time.

10 Can**'**t you see he**'**s not doing the invoices accurately?

11 The weather**'**s been great throughout the holiday.

12 The team members**'** enthusiasm helped them do their best.

13 The dog chased its tail for half an hour.

14 The children ran right up to the water**'**s edge.

15 It**'**s got to have its claws clipped.

Exercise on page 90

The Mayor asked the people at the meeting what they thought of wind farms. **H**ands shot up and people offered a range of opinions**:** some said they were ugly**,** others that they made too much noise**,** and a few that they could help slow the rise in sea level**.** **W**hen everyone had said their bit**,** the Mayor spoke again and confirmed the council had agreed to site a wind farm on Golden Hill**.** **T**here were shouts**,** cries and some applause from the audience**,** but silence reigned when he shouted out that the rent from the land would allow the council to build a modern hospital with all the latest equipment for the town.

Answers to exercises in Part C

Exercises on page 94

1 Do you **expect** me to help you mow the lawn?

2 Most students **accept** their results without complaint.

3 He was delighted to **accept** the award for his research.

4 They saw everything in Paris **except** the Eiffel Tower.

5 Do you **accept** that you need to work harder?

6 Please don't **expect** him to bring anything.

7 What do you **expect** if you don't study all year?

8 They chose to **accept** the offer of compensation.

Exercises on page 95

1 I would **advise** you to go to the doctor.

2 They won't listen to my **advice**.

3 Please follow the man's **advice**. He knows what he's talking about.

4 I had to **advise** him not to buy the car.

5 Do you have any **advice** about what to wear to this interview?

6 My **advice** to you is to do what you are told.

7 If they continue to ignore her **advice**, she'll stop helping them.

8 We **advise** all UK citizens to contact the British Embassy.

9 I would **advise** all my students to read regularly.

10 We always **advise** travellers to check what vaccinations they need.

Exercises on page 96

1 His speech had a great **effect** on the children in the audience.

2 The **effect** of water on iron is rust.

3 The Holocaust Exhibition will surely **affect** all who visit it.

4 What **effect** do you get if you splash the walls with red and blue paint?

5 The new documents failed to **affect** the minister's opinion.

6 How does the heat usually **affect** you?

7 The **effect** of prolonged exposure to sunshine is sunburn.

8 For many the **effect** of consuming too much butter is increased levels of cholesterol in the blood.

9 Mosquito bites don't **affect** some people, but others can't stop scratching.

10 Scientists can't agree what **effect** mobile phones have on the brain.

Exercises on page 97

1 They are trying to find an **alternative** to nuclear power.

2 It's not fair if one person does it every week. They should **alternate**.

3 Have you explored every **alternative**?

4 His shirt has **alternate** stripes of pink and pale blue.

5 Sarah favours **alternative** medicine rather than conventional medicines.

6 There should be an **alternative** to chips on the menu.

7 The weather tended to **alternate** between snow and sunshine.

8 They hold gym classes on **alternate** Saturdays.

9 Is there any **alternative** to prison?

10 The boys **alternate** between being rude to us and ignoring us.

Exercises on page 98

1 They came to **our** house.

2 The vet said we could not take **our** cat home.

3 **Are** you ready yet?

4 **Our** potatoes are the best on the allotment.

5 **Are** the courses starting next week?

6 **Our** new courses **are** very popular.

7 There **are** two parks in the city centre.

8 They **are** delighted with the flowers.

9 Where is **our** dinner?

10 Where **are our** friends?

Exercises on page 99

1 She wants to **borrow** my hairdryer.

2 Jane wouldn't **lend** her new fountain pen to her friend.

3 If I **lend** you this book, can you **lend** me your new CD?

4 He asked to **borrow** my casserole dish and never gave it back.

5 Alex was able to **borrow** everything he needed to go camping.

6 Why don't you **lend** him your new torch?

7 Please **lend** me your MP3 player for the journey.

8 He needs to **borrow** money from the bank to open a shop.

9 The bank will **lend** him the money because they know he'll succeed.

10 My grandma used to say, '**Borrow** to save and you'll always have plenty.'

Exercises on page 100

1 What did you buy at the market? I **bought** nothing.

2 For the camping weekend he **brought** lots of things from his larder.

3 How many new computers has the school **bought**?

4 They have **bought** lots of new clothes in the sales.

5 The children **brought** their favourite toys to play with.

6 European explorers **brought** new diseases to South America.

7 They've spent two hours at the shops. What have they **bought**?

8 Have they **brought** their tent with them?

9 I've **brought** some visitors to cheer you up.

10 I can't believe he's **bought** another one from eBay!

Exercises on page 101

1 On a bike it's best to **brake** gently.

2 The doctor has recommended he take a **break** from work.

3 The bus driver had to **brake** to avoid hitting the dog.

4 Taking a weekend **break** abroad has got much cheaper.

5 How did you **break** the lid of that casserole dish?

6 Last year when he went skiing he **broke** his arm.

7 I've been working on this for hours and I need a **break**.

8 He **braked** suddenly when he saw the police car ahead.

Exercises on page 102

1 He ran out of **breath** after the first lap.

2 When they found the missing keys I heard them **breathe** a sigh of relief.

3 The doctor told him to take a deep **breath**.

4 You can help stop yourself falling asleep if you take a deep **breath**.

5 The children measured the **breadth** and the height of their tent.

6 It can be difficult to **breathe** when you're wearing a mask.

7 They could scarcely **breathe** because the smoke was so thick.

8 How long can you hold your **breath** under water?

Exercises on page 103

1 Where's the ball? It's over **here**.

2 Can you **hear** me at the back?

3 I didn't **hear** what you said.

4 They'll **hear** you if you speak clearly.

5 **Here** comes John.

6 The letters to the school are **here**.

7 They don't like living **here**.

8 If you keep talking I won't **hear** what they're saying on the radio.

9 **Here** are the last letters for you to sign.

10 We need to stick to the **here** and now.

Exercises on page 104

1 **It's** been a lovely holiday.

2 The house is too small and **its** garden is too big.

3 **It's** not something I would ever consider.

4 The monster approached. **Its** head was green and slimy.

5 **It's** never too late to learn something new.

6 **It's** a disaster.

7 This book is great. **It's** all about the Pacific Ocean.

8 James says **it's** best to arrive before 10 o'clock.

9 The house was horrid. **Its** walls were painted yucky green.

10 **It's** never going to be ready on time.

Exercises on page 105

1 They've applied for a **licence** to stay open late.

2 This **licence** allows you to serve alcohol daily between 7 and 11pm.

3 They granted him a **licence** to fish on the River Test.

4 The premises were first **licensed** 40 years ago.

5 Do you have to be **licensed** to sell certain chemicals?

6 Apply for your new driving **licence** now.

7 If you don't have a TV **licence**, you're bound to be caught.

8 Have you got a **licence** to drive that lorry?

9 The police decided not to renew the bar's **licence**.

10 The bar had applied to be **licensed** to serve alcohol 24 hours a day.

Exercises on page 106

1 Why don't you **lie** and relax on the sofa for half an hour?

2 He **laid** the map out on the car bonnet and studied the route.

3 The geese have **laid** their eggs early this year.

4 Even the best **laid** plans don't always work!

5 They picked up the baby and then **laid** him gently down in his cot.

6 How long have you **lain** there?

7 How long did you **lie** there before the ambulance came?

8 He forgot to **lay** a place at the table for Fred.

9 Please let me **lie** here a little longer.

10 They opened up the kit and **laid** the instruction sheet on the ground.

Exercises on page 107

1 He struck a match and **lit** the night lights.

2 They **lit** the barbeque in plenty of time to cook the food.

3 How many **lighted** candles were there on his cake?

4 How is the hall **lit**?

5 They **lit** the bonfire all around its base.

6 It is dangerous to play with **lighted** matches.

7 The moon **lit** the surface of the water.

8 Never return to a firework after you have **lit** it.

9 She **lit** another cigarette.

10 Keith was standing in the **lighted** window.

Exercises on page 108

1 Can't you tell if a size 20 is going to be too **loose** for you?

2 The doctor has said they need to go on a diet and **lose** a few kilos.

3 If you **lose** your birth certificate it takes ages to replace it.

4 He was driving along and the engine started to **lose** power.

5 I prefer **loose** leaf tea to tea bags.

6 Her muscles are very **loose** from all the yoga she does.

7 He was determined not to **lose** the car keys.

8 I'm not going to **lose** any sleep over it.

9 She always has some **loose** change in her purse.

10 If they keep shouting, George will **lose** it completely.

Exercises on page 109

1 Do you **know** what time it is?

2 I'm sorry, but I can't do it **now**.

3 Did they say you could start now? **No**, they didn't.

4 You should already **know** the difference between right and wrong.

5 Do you **know** the answer? **No**, I don't.

6 When do you finish work? **Now**. I'm getting ready to leave.

7 How did he **know** you were late?

8 There is **no** butter left.

Exercises on page 110

1 He took the top **off** the bottle with his new corkscrew.

2 He put a ribbon around the top **of** the bottle.

3 The recipe needs a kilo **of** flour.

4 They must **have** sold the cottage.

5 He could **have** told me you didn't want to go.

6 Get **off** the table or you'll fall.

7 Sarah might **have** told them the secret.

8 They couldn't **have** got there first.

Exercises on page 111

1 He needs to **practise** regularly to improve his guitar playing.

2 The **practice** of bear-baiting was outlawed only a century ago.

3 There is a football **practice** after school.

4 They had to **practise** for the concert for weeks.

5 This tennis **practice** has not helped him get rid of his problems serving.

6 I haven't decided whether to go to the **practice** this week.

7 John needs to **practise** making scones.

8 My grandma always said, '**Practice** makes perfect!'

9 My father always says, '**Practise** what you preach!'

10 If you **practise**, your playing will improve.

Exercises on page 112

1 He's **quite** unhappy when he goes into kennels.

2 Be **quiet**. You're making too much noise.

3 The children are playing in the park, so the house is **quiet**.

4 He's **quite** friendly and always waves when he sees me.

5 Teachers like the class to be **quiet** while they take the register.

6 He was **quite** calm immediately after the accident.

7 He said the film was **quite** good so I'd like to see it.

8 I think that's **quite** unfair.

9 I'm sure you can be really **quiet** if you try!

10 The engine's so **quiet** I can't hear when I've stalled.

Exercises on page 113

1 I thought the car was **stationary** so I turned right in front of it.

2 Please check who is responsible for **stationery**.

3 The **stationery** cupboard key has gone missing.

4 When cycling watch out for the doors of **stationary** vehicles!

5 They've had the bill for last month's **stationery**.

6 The customs officials asked them to remain **stationary**.

7 I couldn't tell from that distance whether the car was **stationary** or not.

8 Make a list of all the **stationery** you need for your department.

9 Never cross the road between two **stationary** vehicles.

10 Put the **stationery** order in by the 10th of every month.

Exercises on page 114

1 **There** aren't any chocolates left.

2 **There** are six doughnuts on the plate.

3 **Their** decision not to come seems odd.

4 They live in London, but **their** parents live in Devon.

5 I'm not sure why **they're** not here yet.

6 **There** were many articles about it in the press.

7 **They're** going to buy a new PC.

8 He says **their** car is too old to fix.

Exercises on page 115

1 They **threw** their old sofa out.

2 I dropped the ball even **though** he **threw** it to me gently.

3 They'll go **through** the motions but they won't actually do anything.

4 They are determined to stay together **through** thick and thin.

5 **Though** he's short he can still reach the shelf.

6 They ran **through** the tunnel at top speed.

7 He **threw** the ball into the crowd.

8 The programme plays music **through** the night.

Exercises on page 116

1 I'm going **to** help him tomorrow.

2 They can't fit in the car **too**.

3 There are **too** many people coming to the party.

4 How many glasses are there on the table? **Two**.

5 **To** get to London by 10 o'clock you need **to** take the 8.50 train.

6 He was **too** hasty so he missed the most important clues.

7 Why doesn't she buy one **too**? They're such a bargain.

8 It's **too** late. The train's already left.

Exercises on page 117

1 They lived **where** they could find work.

2 **We're** too old to retrain.

3 **Wear** whatever you like to the party.

4 **Where** is my diary?

5 **We're** very happy to see you!

6 Why **were** they standing in front of the screen?

Exercises on page 118

1 He's the boy **whose** mum works at the hospital.

2 **Whose** books are those?

3 **Whose** decision will that be?

4 **Who's** coming to the meeting?

5 **Who's** finished their work?

6 That's the manager **whose** team got the special award.

7 Can you tell me **whose** jacket you like best?

8 Do you know **who's** on the interview panel?

9 'Those aren't my books.' **'Whose** are they then?'

10 Why can't you tell me **whose** money it is?

Answers to exercises in Part D

Exercises on page 147

1 Lynne assumed that they'd be on time.

2 He expected that they would help.

3 The committee found it hard to decide.

4 They completed the roadworks in July.

5 They investigated the accusations.

6 The school has arranged for the children to attend the concert.

7 They wanted to discuss the problem.

8 The team has announced the new start date.

Exercises on page 150

Exercise 1

The dentist was exasperated by patients failing to pay for their treatment on time and failing to show up for appointments. As a result he decided to take drastic measures by refusing to see any patients who did this and removing them permanently from his list. (21 words + 25 words)

Exercise 2

The minister claimed to agree in principle with the opinion expressed earlier that day by his colleague. But, when quizzed about it by other politicians and the press, he seemed unable to express that opinion clearly in his own words. (17 words + 23 words)

Exercises on page 162

Exercise 1

They decided to leave the island and head for home a week or **two** early. Chris had been happy to play tennis with her **friends** up until the**n**, but she'd become keen to leave as soon as they ran out of money.

Exercise 2

Some people say that texting on mobile phones will become the new way to write. Not for many years I'd say! I imagine you've heard about the 13-year-old **Scottish** schoolgirl who shocked her teachers by writing an essay entirely **in** text message shorthand. She did**n't** get a very good grade. Did you know that the first text message was sent in December **1992**, but that it didn't really have a **big** following until the early 2000s**?** Every hour in the **UK** over two million text messages are sent and in 2003 on New **Y**ear's **D**ay over 100 million **were** sent.

Exercise on page 163

Dear Sir/Madam

Request for extension to parking permits for Brown[1] Street, Durham

I enclose a **petition**[2] from the majority of residents of Brown Street requesting you extend our parking permit hours from 6pm to 10pm.

I'd like to explain why the current permit finishing at 6pm is a problem. The residential properties in Brown Street **are**[3] in the centre of town near restaurants, clubs and bars. After 6pm **our street**[4] provides free and convenient parking to people who work in the bars and those who socialize there.

When residents get home from work they often cannot park **in**[5] Brown Street and have to pay to park further away. This means they have to pay to park further away from their homes and then struggle with their heavy shopping to their front doors.

Please let me know what we need **to**[6] do to progress this request. I will be happy to supply any further information you require. I look forward to hearing from you soon – my phone number is 03645 789456.

Yours faithfully

Lynne Walker
Brown Street residents' representative

Notes

1. If you missed this it could be because you didn't look at the heading at all.
2. Spelling mistake: a spellchecker would find this. Did you?
3. You need *are* to agree with the subject *residential properties*.
4. The word *it* doesn't refer back to anything in the previous sentence, so we need to write *our street* to make it clear.
5. A spellchecker would spot this double word. Well done if you spotted it. That means you really are looking at every word on the page. If you didn't see it I imagine you weren't reading the words aloud as you pointed at them.
6. Did you spot this missing word? You needed to be reading and concentrating to see it was missing.

Answers to exercises in Part E

Exercises on page 173

(These are just possible versions of the sort of thing you might have written.)

Exercise 1

Hi Sarah

I've finished all the folders up to and including surnames beginning with T. Could you continue with S and leave me a note to say where you finish.

Many thanks

Rachel

Exercise 2

4 May 2006

Dear Mr Smith

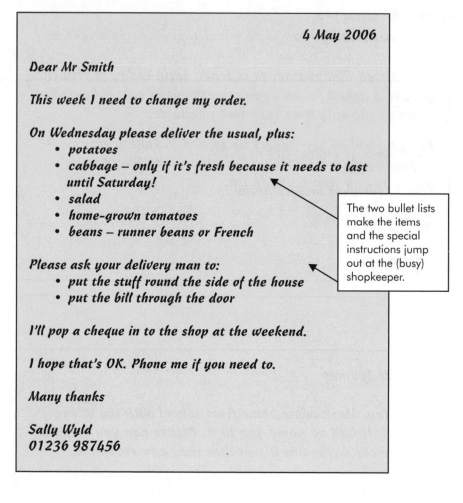

This week I need to change my order.

On Wednesday please deliver the usual, plus:

- *potatoes*
- *cabbage – only if it's fresh because it needs to last until Saturday!*
- *salad*
- *home-grown tomatoes*
- *beans – runner beans or French*

Please ask your delivery man to:

- *put the stuff round the side of the house*
- *put the bill through the door*

I'll pop a cheque in to the shop at the weekend.

I hope that's OK. Phone me if you need to.

Many thanks

Sally Wyld
01236 987456

The two bullet lists make the items and the special instructions jump out at the (busy) shopkeeper.

Exercise 3

> *Dear Mrs Dobory*
>
> *I am afraid Philippa needs to leave early today to visit the dentist. I asked for an appointment out of school hours but this was the only time they had available.*
>
> *I will come to collect her at 3.20.*
>
> *Thanks for your understanding.*
>
> *Best wishes*
>
> *Jane Franklin*

Exercise 4

> *Dear Mr Thomas*
>
> *Yesterday, Mark came home from school with the wrong sweater. It had no name-tag in it. Please can you help him find the child who has his so that they can exchange.*
>
> *Thank you*
>
> *Jane Dodsom*

Exercises on page 176

(These are just possible versions of the sort of thing you might have written.)

Exercise 1

Food

- Savoury
  - Sandwiches – cheese, salad, chicken
  - Hard boiled eggs
  - Crisps
- Sweet
  - Fruit
  - Cake

Drink

- For adults
- For children

Other essentials

- Cutlery
- Glasses
- Blankets to sit on
- Deckchairs

Sports stuff

- Cricket set
- Balls for volleyball / football
- Tennis / badminton rackets
- Rounders bat

Exercise 2

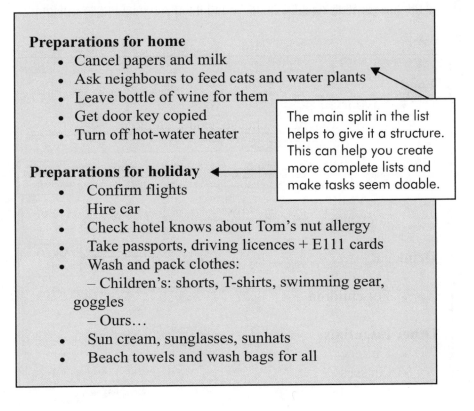

Preparations for home

- Cancel papers and milk
- Ask neighbours to feed cats and water plants
- Leave bottle of wine for them
- Get door key copied
- Turn off hot-water heater

Preparations for holiday

- Confirm flights
- Hire car
- Check hotel knows about Tom's nut allergy
- Take passports, driving licences + E111 cards
- Wash and pack clothes:
  – Children's: shorts, T-shirts, swimming gear, goggles
  – Ours…
- Sun cream, sunglasses, sunhats
- Beach towels and wash bags for all

The main split in the list helps to give it a structure. This can help you create more complete lists and make tasks seem doable.

Exercises on page 182

(These are just possible versions of the sort of thing you might have written.)

Exercise 1

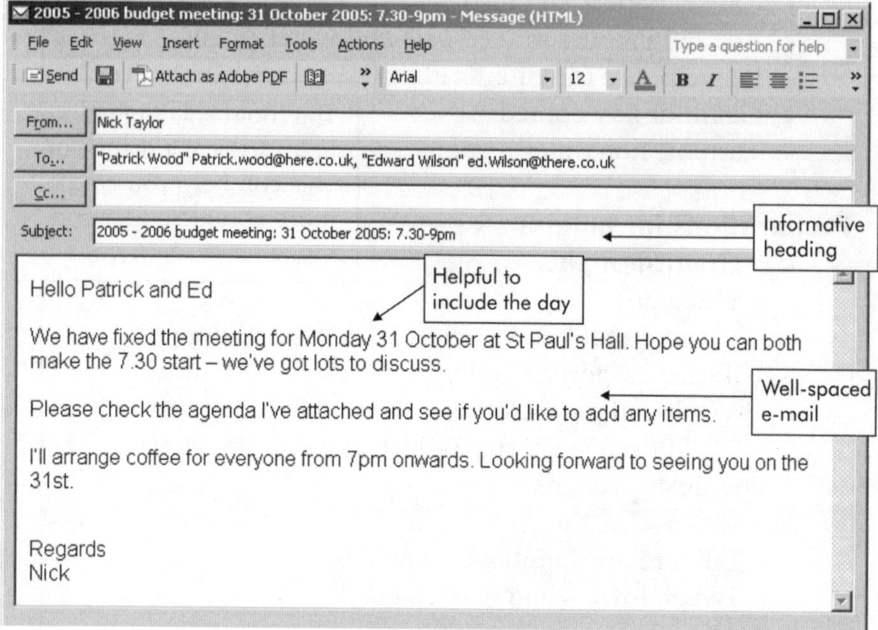

2005 - 2006 budget meeting: 31 October 2005: 7.30-9pm - Message (HTML)
File Edit View Insert Format Tools Actions Help
Type a question for help
Send
Attach as Adobe PDF
Arial
12
From...
Nick Taylor
To...
"Patrick Wood" Patrick.wood@here.co.uk, "Edward Wilson" ed.Wilson@there.co.uk
Cc...
Subject:
2005 - 2006 budget meeting: 31 October 2005: 7.30-9pm
Informative heading
Helpful to include the day
Hello Patrick and Ed
We have fixed the meeting for Monday 31 October at St Paul's Hall. Hope you can both make the 7.30 start – we've got lots to discuss.
Well-spaced e-mail
Please check the agenda I've attached and see if you'd like to add any items.
I'll arrange coffee for everyone from 7pm onwards. Looking forward to seeing you on the 31st.
Regards
Nick

Exercise 2

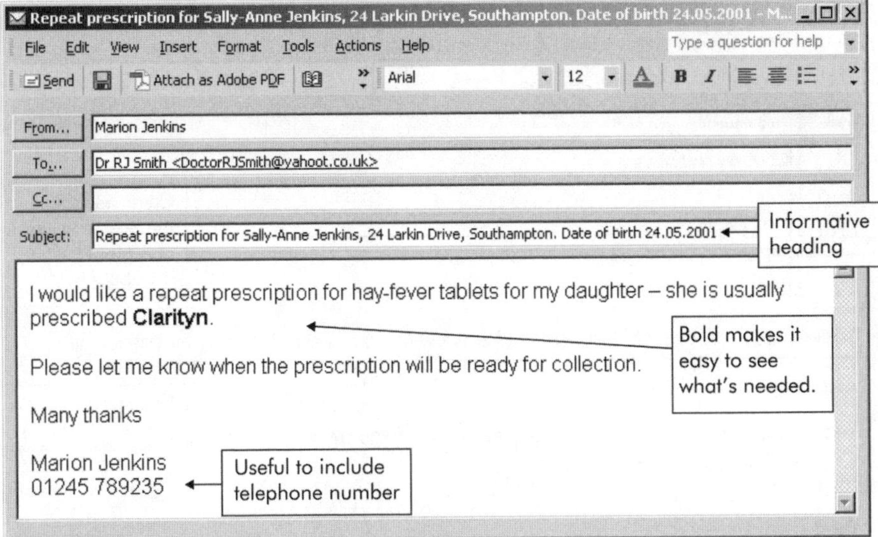

Repeat prescription for Sally-Anne Jenkins, 24 Larkin Drive, Southampton. Date of birth 24.05.2001 - M...
File Edit View Insert Format Tools Actions Help
Type a question for help
Send
Attach as Adobe PDF
Arial
12
From...
Marion Jenkins
To...
Dr RJ Smith <DoctorRJSmith@yahoot.co.uk>
Cc...
Subject:
Repeat prescription for Sally-Anne Jenkins, 24 Larkin Drive, Southampton. Date of birth 24.05.2001
Informative heading
I would like a repeat prescription for hay-fever tablets for my daughter – she is usually prescribed **Clarityn**.
Bold makes it easy to see what's needed.
Please let me know when the prescription will be ready for collection.
Many thanks
Marion Jenkins
01245 789235
Useful to include telephone number

Exercise 3

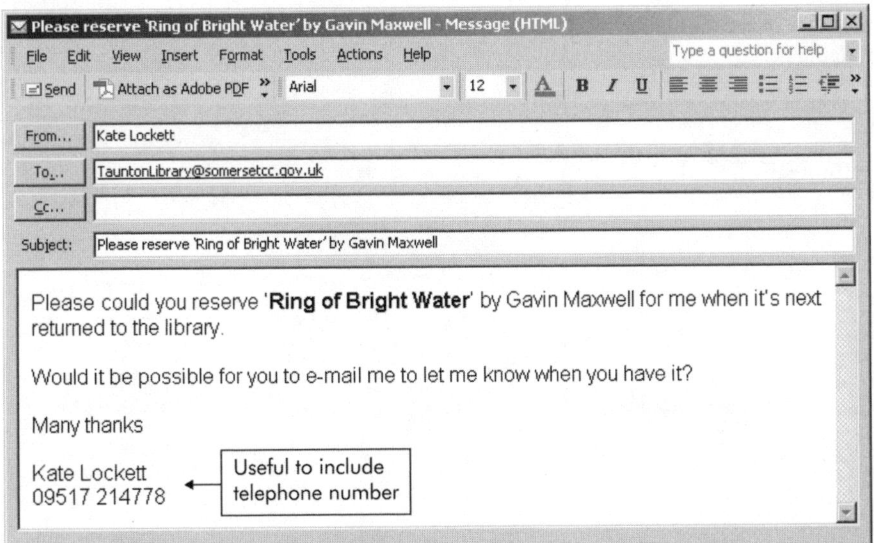

Please reserve 'Ring of Bright Water' by Gavin Maxwell - Message (HTML)
File Edit View Insert Format Tools Actions Help
Type a question for help
Send
Attach as Adobe PDF
Arial
12
From...
Kate Lockett
To...
TauntonLibrary@somersetcc.gov.uk
Cc...
Subject:
Please reserve 'Ring of Bright Water' by Gavin Maxwell
Please could you reserve '**Ring of Bright Water**' by Gavin Maxwell for me when it's next returned to the library.
Would it be possible for you to e-mail me to let me know when you have it?
Many thanks
Kate Lockett
09517 214778
Useful to include telephone number

Exercise 4

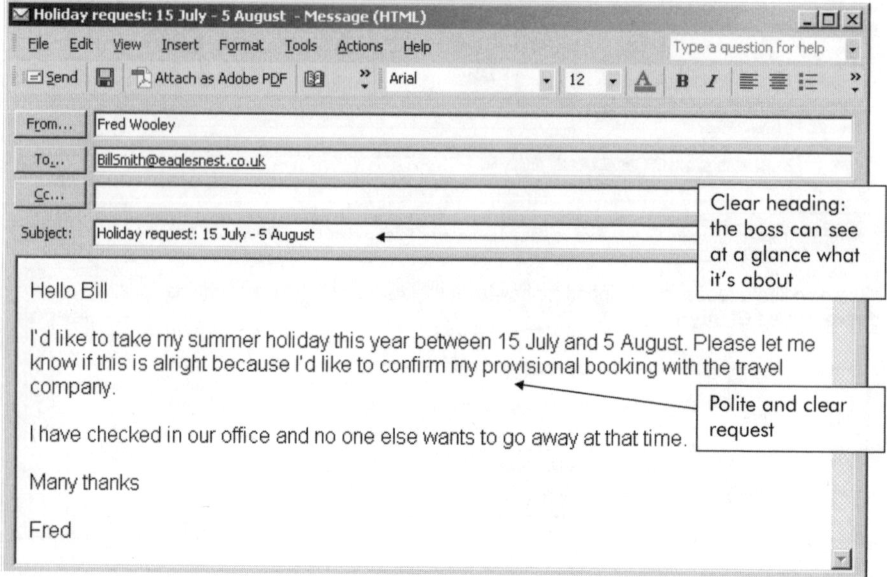
Holiday request: 15 July - 5 August - Message (HTML)

From... Fred Wooley

To... BillSmith@eaglesnest.co.uk

Cc...

Subject: Holiday request: 15 July - 5 August

Hello Bill

I'd like to take my summer holiday this year between 15 July and 5 August. Please let me know if this is alright because I'd like to confirm my provisional booking with the travel company.

I have checked in our office and no one else wants to go away at that time.

Many thanks

Fred

Exercise 5

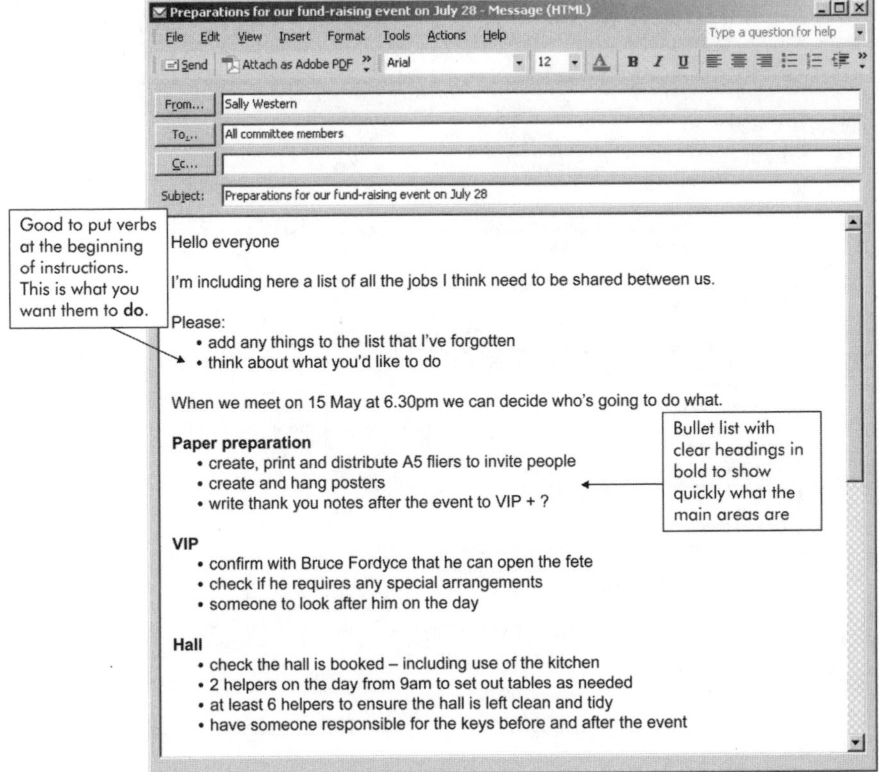

continued over...

Preparations for our fund-raising event on July 28 - Message (HTML)
File Edit View Insert Format Tools Actions Help
Type a question for help
Send Attach as Adobe PDF Arial 12
From... Sally Western
To... All committee members
Cc...
Subject: Preparations for our fund-raising event on July 28
Good to put verbs at the beginning of instructions. This is what you want them to **do**.
Hello everyone
I'm including here a list of all the jobs I think need to be shared between us.
Please:
• add any things to the list that I've forgotten
• think about what you'd like to do
When we meet on 15 May at 6.30pm we can decide who's going to do what.
Bullet list with clear headings in bold to show quickly what the main areas are
Paper preparation
• create, print and distribute A5 fliers to invite people
• create and hang posters
• write thank you notes after the event to VIP + ?
VIP
• confirm with Bruce Fordyce that he can open the fete
• check if he requires any special arrangements
• someone to look after him on the day
Hall
• check the hall is booked – including use of the kitchen
• 2 helpers on the day from 9am to set out tables as needed
• at least 6 helpers to ensure the hall is left clean and tidy
• have someone responsible for the keys before and after the event

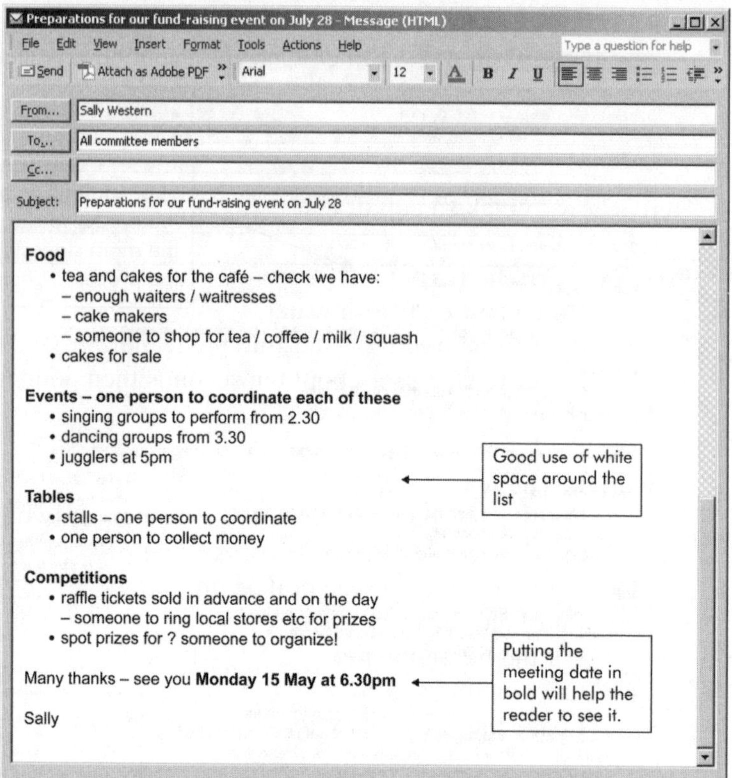

Preparations for our fund-raising event on July 28 - Message (HTML)

From... Sally Western

To... All committee members

Cc...

Subject: Preparations for our fund-raising event on July 28

Food

- tea and cakes for the café – check we have:
  - enough waiters / waitresses
  - cake makers
  - someone to shop for tea / coffee / milk / squash
- cakes for sale

Events – one person to coordinate each of these

- singing groups to perform from 2.30
- dancing groups from 3.30
- jugglers at 5pm

Tables

- stalls – one person to coordinate
- one person to collect money

Competitions

- raffle tickets sold in advance and on the day
  - someone to ring local stores etc for prizes
- spot prizes for ? someone to organize!

Many thanks – see you **Monday 15 May at 6.30pm**

Sally

Good use of white space around the list
Putting the meeting date in bold will help the reader to see it.

Exercises on page 187

(These are just possible versions of the sort of thing you might have written.)

Exercise 1

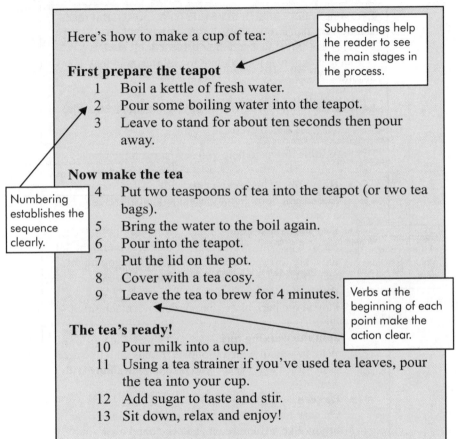

Here's how to make a cup of tea:

Subheadings help the reader to see the main stages in the process.

First prepare the teapot

1 Boil a kettle of fresh water.
2 Pour some boiling water into the teapot.
3 Leave to stand for about ten seconds then pour away.

Now make the tea

Numbering establishes the sequence clearly.

4 Put two teaspoons of tea into the teapot (or two tea bags).
5 Bring the water to the boil again.
6 Pour into the teapot.
7 Put the lid on the pot.
8 Cover with a tea cosy.
9 Leave the tea to brew for 4 minutes.

Verbs at the beginning of each point make the action clear.

The tea's ready!

10 Pour milk into a cup.
11 Using a tea strainer if you've used tea leaves, pour the tea into your cup.
12 Add sugar to taste and stir.
13 Sit down, relax and enjoy!

Exercise 2

Be safe on the roads! ← Clear heading with the main purpose of the instructions

Everyone wants children to be safe on the roads. But roads can be very dangerous. Cars, buses, lorries and even bicycles can travel fast and their drivers don't always pay as much attention as they should to children who may be around.

Sometimes children may not be paying attention when they walk to and from school.

Here are some things to help you stay safe on the roads:

- **Remember the green cross code** ← Subheadings with the main points in bold
  Look right, look left and right again before you cross a road. ← Command form of the verb to make the action clear
- **Use your senses!**
  As well as your eyes, use your ears … you might not see a big lorry just round the corner, but you might hear it! Using your senses makes sense.
- **Don't play on the road**
  Play in the park or in your garden, it's much safer there.
- **Join the walking bus**
  Walk to school with a group of friends who live near you. Mums and Dads could take turns walking with you.
- **Be seen**
  On dark mornings and afternoons wear something bright, like a fluorescent jacket or band over your uniform so you can be seen more easily.

Exercise 3

Dear __________

Bouncy Castle safety notes

Thank you so much for volunteering to man (person?!) the Bouncy Castle this afternoon.

Here's what you need to do:

To keep the children safe:

Verbs at the beginning of each instruction – do this!

- Make children take their shoes off before getting on the castle.
- Allow a maximum of 10 children on the castle at any one time.
- Make each session five minutes.
- For each session allow only children from the same age group.
  I suggest: Up to 4 years
  4 – 8 years
  9 – 12 years
- Watch them as they bounce!
- Check the castle stays inflated – see the valve at the back.
- Ring the caretaker Bill on 07891 22453 for help if it starts to go too squashy.

Bullet points are gathered under two separate subheadings. This avoids a long list of bullets where some points might get lost.

Don'ts

Don't allow repeated for emphasis

- Don't allow the children to dive bomb each other.
- Don't allow them to push each other off the castle.
- Don't allow them to sit on the side walls of the castle.
- Don't allow them to eat or drink when on the castle.

Again many thanks

Caroline
PTA person

Exercises on page 196

(These are just possible versions of the sort of thing you might have written.)

Exercise 1

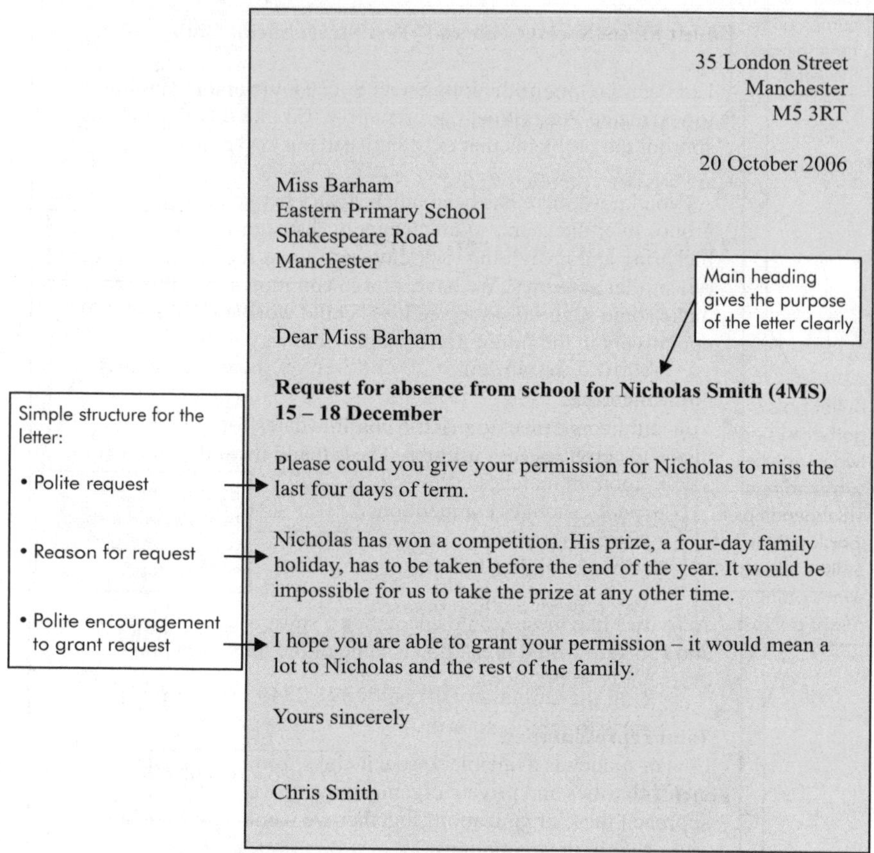

35 London Street
Manchester
M5 3RT

20 October 2006

Miss Barham
Eastern Primary School
Shakespeare Road
Manchester

Dear Miss Barham

Request for absence from school for Nicholas Smith (4MS) 15 – 18 December

Please could you give your permission for Nicholas to miss the last four days of term.

Nicholas has won a competition. His prize, a four-day family holiday, has to be taken before the end of the year. It would be impossible for us to take the prize at any other time.

I hope you are able to grant your permission – it would mean a lot to Nicholas and the rest of the family.

Yours sincerely

Chris Smith

Main heading gives the purpose of the letter clearly
Simple structure for the letter:
• Polite request
• Reason for request
• Polite encouragement to grant request

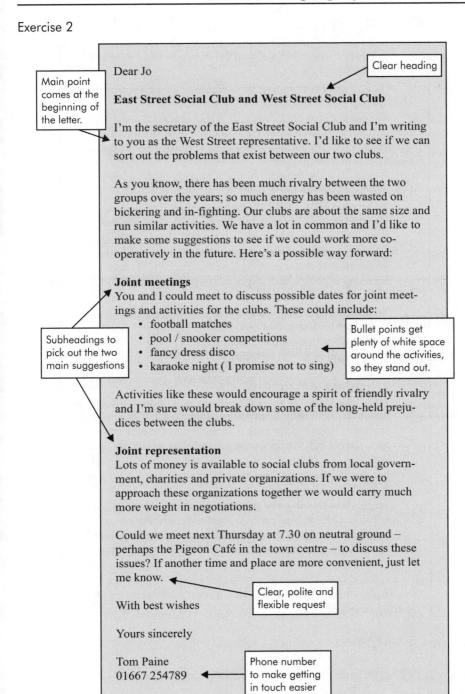

Exercise 2

Dear Jo

East Street Social Club and West Street Social Club

I'm the secretary of the East Street Social Club and I'm writing to you as the West Street representative. I'd like to see if we can sort out the problems that exist between our two clubs.

As you know, there has been much rivalry between the two groups over the years; so much energy has been wasted on bickering and in-fighting. Our clubs are about the same size and run similar activities. We have a lot in common and I'd like to make some suggestions to see if we could work more co-operatively in the future. Here's a possible way forward:

Joint meetings
You and I could meet to discuss possible dates for joint meetings and activities for the clubs. These could include:

- football matches
- pool / snooker competitions
- fancy dress disco
- karaoke night (I promise not to sing)

Activities like these would encourage a spirit of friendly rivalry and I'm sure would break down some of the long-held prejudices between the clubs.

Joint representation
Lots of money is available to social clubs from local government, charities and private organizations. If we were to approach these organizations together we would carry much more weight in negotiations.

Could we meet next Thursday at 7.30 on neutral ground – perhaps the Pigeon Café in the town centre – to discuss these issues? If another time and place are more convenient, just let me know.

With best wishes

Yours sincerely

Tom Paine
01667 254789

Exercise 3

Dear Councillor Taylor

Help set up a safe social centre for young people

I am a concerned resident living in the city centre. I don't have children myself, but I know I would be very worried if I had teenagers and lived here.

I see two main problems:

1. Nowhere for 14–18 year olds to hang out

Up until around 14 years old they can go to the various youth groups around the city. After that, there is nothing for them to do except try to sneak into pubs. I see groups of young people in the evenings, particularly Friday and Saturday nights, wandering aimlessly in hordes around the town. If they do have an aim, it seems to be to get drunk.

Suggestions to solve the problem

- Set up clubs specifically for this age group where they can gather to chat, and listen to music.
- Set up more sports facilities.

2. Nowhere to skateboard safely

Teenagers are still skateboarding day and night in the car park near the leisure centre. It is dangerous for them and any one else in the car park. I thought that the new board park the council set up would get them out of the car park, but they're still there. They say that the new park is great – but that it's for bikes (BMX – I think they said) and it's **not suitable** for skateboards.

Suggestion to solve the problem

- Build a skateboard park. Skateboarding is not a five-minute wonder; I've seen children skateboarding for years now. We should encourage them by giving them the right facilities.

Please give these suggestions your support. I look forward to hearing from you.

Yours sincerely

Jane Grant

Glossary of Language Terms

Some of the words you may come across in this book are special terms to describe language and how it is used. Some of them may be unfamiliar. This glossary explains what they mean.

adjective

An adjective is a word that tells you something about a noun. For example, *difficult*, *good* and *stupid* are adjectives: *a **difficult** sum* • *That film was **good**.* • *a **stupid** mistake*

adverb

An adverb is a word that tells you something about verbs, adjectives or other adverbs. For example, *badly*, *abroad* and *really* are adverbs: *He played **badly**.* • *I lived **abroad**.* • *I am **really** sorry.* • *He played **really badly**.*

future

The future tense of a verb is the form that you use when you are talking about something that has still to happen. Usually, the future tense is made up of more than one word. For example, *will finish* in *I **will finish** the job next week* is a future tense form of the verb *finish*.

negative

A negative is a word or phrase that means 'not' or 'no'. For example, *I am **not** ready*.

noun

A noun is a word that refers to a person or a thing. For example, *tree*, *Sue* and *idea* are nouns.

object

The object is the word or words in a sentence that stand for the person or thing that the verb affects. For example, *it* is the object in the sentence ***He** ate it*.

past

The past tense of a verb is the form that you use when you are talking about what has happened before now. For example, *relaxed* in *I **relaxed** after the race* is a past tense form of the verb *relax*.

phrase

A phrase is a group of words expressing a single meaning or idea. A phrase might be used on its own or as part of a sentence. For example, *now and then* in *I go swimming* ***now and then*** is a phrase.

plural

A plural is the form of a word that you use when there is more than one person, thing or group. For example, *families* is the plural of *family*.

possessive

A possessive is a word that shows who or what a person or thing belongs to. For example, *my*, *yours* and *theirs*, and nouns with *'s* added at the end, are possessives.

present

The present tense of a verb is the form that you use when you are talking about what is happening here and now. For example, *throw* and *throws* in *I* ***throw*** *the ball and he* ***throws*** *it back* are present tense forms of the verb *throw*.

pronoun

A pronoun is a word that can be used in place of a noun. For example, in the sentence *Gary ate the ice cream*, *Gary* and *the ice cream* could be changed to pronouns and the sentence would be ***He*** *ate* ***it***.

punctuation

Punctuation is the process of putting in special marks such as commas and full stops in writing to mark off pauses or breaks in what has been written.

question

A question is a type of sentence that you use when you want to know the answer to something. You write a question mark (**?**) after a sentence that is a question.

sentence

A sentence is a sequence of words that includes a verb and expresses a statement a question or a command.

singular

A singular is the form of a word that you use when there is one person, thing or group, rather than two or more. For example, the singular of *buses* is *bus*.

subject

The subject of a sentence is the word (or words) that stands before the verb and controls the verb. The subject usually stands for the person or thing doing the action of the verb. For example, *he* is the subject in the sentence ***He** ate it*.

verb

A verb is the word in a sentence that tells you what someone or something does. For example, *be*, *eat* and *speak* are verbs.

Index